DISTILLED
IN
CHICAGO

DISTILLED

IN

CHICAGO

A HISTORY

DAVID WITTER

AMERICAN PALATE

Published by American Palate
A Division of The History Press
Charleston, SC
www.historypress.com

Front cover photos by David Witter. Back cover distillery photo courtesy of KOVAL Distilleries. Atlas Bar photo courtesy of William Kralovec.

First published 2022

Manufactured in the United States

ISBN 9781467152280

Library of Congress Control Number: 2022943534

CONTENTS

PREFACE

I was first introduced to the world of alcohol and spirits through my grandfather's tavern. Anthony Kazlauskas owned and ran a bar on Grant Street in Gary, Indiana, for forty years. Like most immigrants, he came to America with little—"twenty five dollars and a few pairs of socks." He worked for a time in the steel mills, but although he was not educated, he noticed how much the men drank before, after and between shifts. Selling them drinks was a lot easier than working in the mills, so with much industry, he saved and opened his bar, the Kaunas Tavern, named after his hometown in Lithuania.

He worked six days a week. I have hazy memories of going to the bar. Usually my mom and my dad would drive by on our way back home to Chicago. He was always at the bar, and that was sometimes the only way my mom, his daughter, could see him. We usually did not spend much time there, and I was often made to wait outside in the car during the visit.

But I have much stronger memories of my grandparents' house. I was somewhat of a sickly child and I guess a bit more work than most, so I spent much time there, being looked after by my extended family. Since my conditions sometimes kept me from going outside, the house became my play area. The basement especially was a place I could explore. It was large, with a smooth cement floor, but it was very musty. In the back areas, there was a large, freestanding wooden shed or pen. There was always a hasp and padlock on it, so it remained a mystery. That is, until the day I found it open. I looked inside, and there were piled boxes and boxes and boxes packed with

My grandfather Anthony Kazlauskas (*left behind bar*) owned the Kaunas Tavern in Gary, Indiana. *Author's collection.*

bottles. One of the boxes was open. I lifted the box top and saw that it was filled with distilled spirits. But these were not your everyday spirits.

I have strong memories of opening the box and pulling out a pint of Du Bouchett Peppermint Schnapps. Made from distilled spirits, peppermint or peppermint flavorings and a great deal of sweetener, it was a favorite drink in many ethnic households, as well as with teenagers and homeless men (who were in those days called "bums"). Since my grandfather owned a bar that catered mainly to eastern European ethnics and "bums," I never saw any Johnny Walker Scotch, Old Grand Dad Bourbon or Gilbey's Gin stored in his basement. In fact, there were no whiskeys, gins or rums. Instead, I saw Mar-Salle's Blackberry Brandy, Mar-Salle Pelinkovac, Mar-Salle Cherry Liqueur and plenty of Du Bouchett's schnapps and Blanc Sloe Gin, all packed away in corrugated boxes in my grandfather's basement. There were so many boxes that I now believe my grandfather may have also worked as a Gary-area distributor for these Chicago-made concoctions. The blackberry brandy, Pelinkovac and cherry liquor are all knockoffs of aperitifs that were part of the culture and tradition of southern and eastern Europeans—Serbians, Hungarians, Poles, Slovaks and Lithuanians, of which there were plenty working in the mills, factories and refineries of south Chicago and northwest Indiana. The Chicago businessmen who made them, as well as my grandfather, knew that by selling them they were offering not only alcoholic relaxation but also a reminder of a faraway homeland. The sloe gin really has nothing to do with gin but rather is another sugary drink often made into "sloe-gin fizzes."

It is odd how young childhood memories work, but the labels, with their colorful pictures of fruit, also stuck in my brain. As an adult, I would see these labels at various antique stores and in collections of ephemera and start to buy them. You will see many of these labels later in the book. Many years after my grandfather, grandmother and later uncles passed on, I was charged with the grim task of beginning to remove their belongings from the basement. One of the first things I found was a pint bottle of the peppermint schnapps. It had probably been there since my grandfather sold the tavern around 1970. I began to wonder about not only the history of that bottle, on whose bottom was written, "Prepared and Bottled by Many, Blanc, Chicago, Illinois," but also the history of all the spirits that were made (or as I later learned, *not made*) in Chicago.

CHICAGO, A CITY THAT MADE BEER BUT NOT WHISKEY

Chicago has always been associated with beer. Early brewers like William Ogden, Frederick and Charles Wacker, Michael Diversey, Conrad Sulzer and William Lill became civic leaders and have streets, parks and schools named after them. By the late 1800s, a host of Chicago "beer barons" had amassed fortunes. They bought and built mansions along "Beer Baron Row" in Wicker Park. Brands like Canadian Ace, Prager, Edelweiss, Atlas, Monarch, Fox De Luxe, Manhattan and Meister Bräu became staples of Chicago's landscape. There have been several books written about beer, brewing and saloons and their influence on Chicago's economy, culture and politics, most notably *Beer: A History of Brewing in Chicago* by Bob Skilnik and *The Saloon: Public Drinking in Boston* by Perry R. Duis. But there has not been a book written specifically about whiskey, rum, gin and other spirits and their history and relationship to Chicago. In its earliest days, it was whiskey and the promise of it in exchange for furs that brought many traders to what would later become Chicago. Whiskey and rum were the economic engines behind the Wolf Tavern, Green Tree Tavern and the Eagle Exchange, the first permanent businesses in Chicago. Whiskey may have also been behind Chicago's first major mob-style extortion tactics and violence against a major business. In 1888, Shufeldt & Company Distilleries was dynamited by what most suspect to be members of the Whiskey Trust. And it was whiskey, gin and rum in many forms that were drunk either by themselves or later alongside beers that became the mainstay for many Chicago saloons.

Spirits, or more primitive forms of them, could be produced at home or farm stills. After wine and mead, there was applejack, which can be made in a simple, passive form by leaving fruits or honey to ferment for a period of time. The yeast from the sugars basically ferments itself into alcohol. In this way, many early settlers were able to make a basic form of distilled spirits. In the seventeenth and eighteenth centuries, almost every family had an uncle, cousin, distant relative, neighbor or friend who made or helped make some sort of distilled spirits. Among many farmers, when it came to making whiskey, there was a saying that went, "Them as didn't would bring their grain to them as did." According to the Distilled Spirits Council, even George Washington made whiskey:

> *George Washington knew all about distilling liquor. He had erected a still at Mount Vernon in the 1770s in order to produce rum but later on, James Anderson, his Scottish plantation manager, is said to have persuaded Washington to plant rye with a mind of producing whiskey. And Washington did, indeed, produce whiskey. During the year before his death in 1799, it is estimated that he earned a considerable profit from his distillery and had over 150 gallons left in storage.*

In many ways, whiskey and beer begin with the same process. There are many different ways to brew beer, and alcohol can be distilled from grains, fruits and other processes. In the end, however, the process and the product are quite different, which may explain part of Chicago's relationship to distilling. Both beverages begin with grain. With whiskey it is usually corn or rye, and with beer it is malted barley, along with corn and other grains. In the making of beer, these grains are first malted, or soaked in water and dried. Grain is then milled or crushed into small pieces. Yeast is added along with hot water to make a mash. Within a brief period, the grain turns into basic sugars, making what brewers call wort. The spent grain is separated from the liquid, which then begins the fermenting process, which in simple ales and stouts may take days to hours, while true lagering, which didn't come to Chicago until the late 1840s, may take months. But with the exception of some modern craft beers that add flavor by aging in barrels, once beer is made, it is ready for consumption.

Whiskey and many other forms of distilled spirits begin in much the same way. In a very basic explanation, grains are malted, milled and made into a mash. Yeast is either added or created naturally, and the mixture is made into a mash and allowed to ferment. With beer and wine, as yeast eats up the sugars, it creates alcohol and carbon dioxide. This method works great for beer, wine and ales, as they are all made so that the final product is milder. Almost all beers, ales and such come in between 4 percent and, at the very highest, 10 percent alcohol, while wines generally top off at 14 to 15 percent ABV. It is at this level that the alcohol becomes toxic for the yeast. To create anything substantially "harder," the maker cannot rely on yeast. To get high alcohol content, the distiller has to physically separate alcohol from water using evaporation and condensation—aka distilling. Although there are many different methods behind distilling, a very simple way to explain distilling as opposed to brewing begins with the fact that water boils at 212 degrees Fahrenheit, while alcohol boils at 173. The primitive home distillers and later Chicago's bootleggers used the most basic method to distill alcohol, known as pot distilling. This is the common image of the copper vessel with more copper tubes running from it like antennas bent into spaghetti. As they are heated, the alcohol vapors rise up into the head of the still; then they are drawn off into an arm and then to a coil. The coil is submerged in cool water, which condenses the alcohol back into liquid. The liquid alcohol runs out of the coil and into a collection vessel.

However, there are many problems with this. The most disturbing is that methanol, or wood alcohol, evaporates at an even lower boiling point of 143 degrees. In many instances, your collecting pot may contain both. Wood alcohol can cause blindness, severe nerve damage or even death. As we will examine in later chapters, Prohibition-era criminal distillers in Chicago and throughout the country made this mistake, sometimes with deadly results. Experienced "bootleggers" and pot distillers can avoid this problem by carefully monitoring the boiling point with thermometers and other tools to make sure that the entire batch is at the 173 degree mark so that the final product is safe. Home- or farm-made whiskey and spirits, carefully made by responsible distillers, will not maim you. But in this simple process, tannins, minerals and other compounds known in the business as "congeners" will end up in your whiskey. Thus, you may get drunk, but the product will look and taste terrible.

This is where column distilling comes in. This method began in the early nineteenth century, or about the same time that the trappers and other folk began mingling with the Native Americans on Wolf Point. Robert Stein made the first pot still or patent still in his native Scotland. This new still consisted of large steel, stainless steel or copper containers that resemble thick test tubes with rounded or pointed tops. This invention changed the world of distilling. Like with beer, early whiskey relied on malt to spur the fermentation process. Column stills allowed Stein to use grains like corn, wheat and rye, which were cheaper and more plentiful, to make whiskey. With these advantages, distillers like Stein could make fifteen thousand gallons of Scotch per year compared to five thousand before. At about the same time, in Ireland, a man named Aeneas Coffey also produced a similar distilling process that he used to make Irish whiskey. Unlike the single pot still, the column still is a tall chamber with several different "pots," each with a plate at the bottom. The plates allow the distiller to stack several little pot stills one on top of the other. Each plate has many holes or perforations at the bottom. The mash, which at this stage is at about 8 percent alcohol, is added at the top of the still. The plates at the bottom begin to heat it. The heat turns the mash into vapors and forces the alcohol to rise up the still. They rise and rise to the different plates. But in between rising, as they enter the new plate or chamber, the alcohol condenses. At each level, sediments like the tannins in the pot still stay behind in the condensation. The vapors rise from chamber to chamber and from plate to plate. This basically distills the same malt mix several times, shedding more tannins and making for a smoother, finer, more consistent whiskey. This process allowed for higher and higher alcohol content and far less work for the distiller because the tannins and impurities are essentially boiled away. The process not only creates cleaner, smoother flavor but also eliminates the need to clean and scour the pot or still after every use.

Johnny Walker began making his first Scotch whiskey in 1825, about three years before Wolf Tavern was opened. Tullamore Dew Irish Whiskey was introduced in 1829. Thus the introduction of mass-produced whiskey pretty much coincides with the settling of Chicago. It also points to the fact that most of the early American whiskey was made by Scots-Irish immigrants. The larger early whiskey producers could be divided into two camps: residents in Maryland and Pennsylvania who used rye to make whiskey—in fact, until the 1990s, Old Overholt's Rye Whiskey was produced in the Monongahela region of Western Pennsylvania—and another group, also of Scots-Irish descent, who used corn, the local crop in states like Kentucky and Tennessee, to make corn whiskey. By the early 1800s, such entrepreneurs as Jacob Beam, Elijah Pepper, Robert Samuels and Basil Hayden were producing early versions of Jim Beam, Old Crow, Maker's Mark and Old Grand Dad, respectively. While beer and especially lager beer were relatively new industries when the German immigrants arrived in Chicago in 1840–50, distilleries in Maryland, Pennsylvania and Kentucky were already established. Or in lay terms, while the

German immigrants were able to introduce the new, cleaner lager beer to Chicago in the 1850s, the Chicago distillers were beaten to the punch. Also, historically, while most every major city had a brewery—St. Louis, Anheuser-Busch; New York, Schaefer; Pittsburg, Iron City; plus all the Milwaukee breweries—distilleries have often tended to settle in rural areas. Thus, while there was still a local demand for whiskey, Chicago did not become a major distiller of spirits. In his *History of Chicago*, Andreas wrote, "In 1864, S.M. Nickerson & Co., Chicago Distillery Co., J.H. Wecker & Co., and W.H. Crosby were the only distillers in the city. Chicago never was much of a distilling city, as the business is decreasing every year."

Yet while Chicago had breweries in almost every neighborhood, the number of distilleries in Chicago dwindled from eight around the time of the Civil War to none by 1890. There are labels and some antique bottles from an outfit called "Sunset Distillery," with a Chicago location and the dates "Since 1894" printed. Yet research on the actual building and address of Sunset Distilling yielded addresses of 343 5th Avenue, 190–92 5th Avenue and 116 5th Avenue, now Wells Street, from the years 1902 to 1917. While they may have produced whiskey, it is also possible that Sunset Liquors was either a front for Peoria's Whiskey Trust or some other type of shell company where liquor was packaged and sold but no spirits were actually distilled. This trend continued for more than one hundred years until 2008, when KOVAL, a small-batch distillery, began making and selling spirits on the open market.

There are many reasons, besides ethnicity and technology, why no whiskey or spirits were distilled in Chicago for almost 150 years. The first is the creation of the National Whiskey Trust in Peoria, Illinois, in the early 1870s. Although the organization will be explained in detail in a later chapter, it worked by combining monopolistic business practices and those of organized crime. The Whiskey Trust bought, priced and even bombed out Chicago's distilleries and controlled much of the nation's whiskey business for nearly 50 years. Organizations like Evanston's Woman's Christian Temperance Union (WCTU) also lobbied to keep distilleries out of area. Prohibition put to rest any plans for resurrecting legal spirits, but "bathtub gin" was definitely produced by both individuals and organized gangs. After Prohibition, the Chicago mob, which controlled much of the local liquor industry, preferred selling and brewing beer, as the higher alcohol content of spirits attracted more heat from "the feds." Perhaps one final reason many spirits were not made in Chicago is population density. Unlike brewing beer, the making of spirits can present many hazards and dangers. The distilled liquid can often reach as high as 95 percent alcohol, making it extremely flammable. Also, especially with larger stills, there is a tremendous amount of pressure, heat and steam going through the condensers. Technological advances in material, construction and some computerized components have made modern stills much safer. But 100 years ago, stills did, and still do, produce tremendous amounts of pressure. The gas vapor, while no longer flammable, is highly combustible, and there have been many, many instances of stills exploding. These types of risks made it far more practical to distill somewhere away from areas with a dense population.

While no spirits were actually produced in Chicago during the postwar period, modern-day empires like those of the Wirtz family, who own the Chicago Blackhawks, took control of the marketing, sales and distribution of brands like Seagram's and are now part of the world's second-largest alcohol conglomerate. Chicago's Kovler family invested heavily in the sales, marketing and distribution of Jim Beam, helping to make it the household name it is today. Much of the profits made from this growth were eventually turned into the Blum Kovler Foundation, which funds arts and other charitable causes in Chicago and throughout the nation. While no spirits were distilled, the post-Prohibition period saw local outfits known as rectifiers buying neutral spirits distilled in the South, adding coloring or flavoring and then bottling them. Some of the locally blended spirits include Dimitri Vodka, Du Bouchett Peppermint Schnapps and imitations of brandies like Pelinkovac, which catered to Chicago's ethnic communities. All the while, a soon-to-become-legendary Swedish drink called Malört was being made in small batches in a back kitchen on Chicago's North Side.

With the explosion of local craft breweries with the new millennium, many small to midsize distilleries like KOVAL, FEW Spirits, CH Distillery, Chicago Distilling and Wolf Point Distilleries have sprung up in Chicagoland. Besides the craft beer movement, new attitudes toward spirits, modern technologies for making them and a more discerning public taste has created a new cottage industry in Chicagoland. From the first whiskey that warmed the cold bodies of trappers on Wolf Point to the temperance movement, Prohibition and the golden age of the gangster; the post-Prohibition magnates who made millions selling, bottling and promoting alcohol; and the modern boutique whiskeys, rums, botanicals and other spirits now being produced in local distilleries, this book tells the story of Chicago, a history distilled.

WOLF POINT

The Birth of Chicago Fueled by Spirits

Wolf Point is the most common name given to the area where the North, South and Main Branches of the Chicago River merge. The point of the intersection of the three bodies of water form a makeshift Y. Combined with a circle, the Y has become the visual symbol of Chicago, placed on municipal vehicles, buildings and bridges. Today, the area around Wolf Point contains some of the most valuable real estate in the city, if not the nation. Nearby buildings include the Merchandise Mart, known for being, after alcohol, a great source of wealth for the Kennedy family. Looking south, there is 333 South Wacker. Sited on a street named after another man—Charles Wacker—who accumulated part of his fortune through brewing, the building resembles a shard of green glass polished and mirrored and stuck into the ground. Other nearby structures include the Trump Tower and Wolf Point Towers, a spectacular mixed-use complex.

Automobile traffic flows along nearby Lake Street, the curving Wacker Drive and across the brick red La Salle Street Bridge. Tour boats, sailboats, bright yellow water taxis, pleasure yachts and flat-bottomed barges churn through the dark-green waters at a steady pace. Railroad tracks also surround the area, taking trains into Union Station from all over the area.

Two hundred years ago, the scene was quite different. It was largely a wetland, filled with cattails, high grass and other native plants and flowers. Waterfowl such as ducks, geese, loons, herons and smaller birds could be seen in abundance, swimming in the still waters and nesting in the tall trees whose roots took in the abundance of fresh water. Beaver, muskrats and

Grave of John Kinzie, father of James Kinzie and one of Chicago's first settlers. *Photo by author.*

other small mammals swam to and fro, their slick brown heads popping out of the water long enough to peer at the shore and find a convenient burrow or nest. Not far away, smoke from the teepees of Potawatomis and other Native Americans could be seen.

This bucolic scene described the area in the late spring, summer, and early fall. Yet as anyone who lives here knows, this is not Chicago. Winter is still an abomination. Summer travelers and revelers can be seen in the sidewalk cafés and the open storefronts of microbreweries enjoying alcohol. But during these months, it is usually "sipped" along with pleasant conversation. This changes come November. Workers rush into taverns or their houses and quickly consume thick ales, whiskeys, cocktails and even stronger beverages like Jepson's Malört, a medicinal concoction that dates back to the days of the Vikings and has become a cult favorite. In short, many Chicagoans drink alcohol to fend off the cold.

Just imagine it is 1828. There is no central heat or any of the other amenities of modern society. Travel is by horse or canoe. The cold Chicago wind blows in off Lake Michigan, unimpeded by any structures. There is no shelter from the driving rain, freezing rain or snow, which blows into dangerous drifts, sometimes several feet high. Coats are made of fur or animal skin and are often heavy. Primitive shoes become frozen blocks of leather. Gloves? Maybe some hide or fur molded into the shape of a hand. In short, if Chicagoans drink to escape the cold today, you can only imagine how pleasurable a warm shot of whiskey was to somebody who had been living outside in the cold for days or even weeks in 1828.

It is in this environment that James Kinzie, the son of early settler John Kinzie, opened Chicago's first business, Wolf Point Tavern. There are several versions as to the origin of its name. The most reasonable is that the area was surrounded by wolves that howled well into the night. Just think how much better a shot of whiskey would taste knowing that you were in a secure structure, safe from the nearby wolves and bears. Legend has it that in 1833, a painted sign was accompanied by a crude picture of a wolf painted on the door. In her book *Wau-Bun: The Early Days of the*

Northwest, Juliette Kinzie described the name as originating from a local character, a Native American named Mo-aw-ay, or wolf, who was a friend of her father. A busy man, Kinzie turned over the management to his friends Billy Caldwell and Samuel Miller. On May 2, 1829, Caldwell and Miller received a tavern license from the Peoria County Commissioners Court with the following stipulations: "Ordered: That a license be granted to Billy Caldwell and Samuel Miller to keep a tavern at Chicago in this state, and that the rates which were allowed heretofore to J.L. Bogardus in the town of Peoria be allowed to the said Caldwell and Miller—and that the Clerk take bond and security to the parties for one hundred dollars— License eight dollars."

The following is a menu and price list for the alcohol served at Wolf Point Tavern. For an outpost on the edge of civilization, the bar list is quite comprehensive:

Each half pint of wine, rum, or brandy…25 cents
Pint…37½ cents
Half Pint of Gin…18¾ cents
Pint of Gin…31¼ cents
Gill of whiskey…6¼ cents
Half Pint of whiskey…12½ cents
Pint of whiskey…18¾ cents
Pint of Cider or Beer…6½ cents
Breakfast, dinner or supper…24 cents
Nights Lodging…12½ cents
Keeping horse overnight on grain or hay…25 cents
The Same as Above, 24 hours…37½ cents

Notice that whiskey is about half the price of gin, wine or rum due to its availability. Minus that, the price ratio of the alcohol is strikingly similar to what you would find in a Chicago corner liquor store. Today, a pint or "40" of decent beer or hard cider runs about five dollars, whereas a pint of better but not top-shelf whiskey runs about fourteen dollars, so the ratio of one-third is about the same. By contrast, a half pint of whiskey costs about as much as a night's lodging. Today, even a lower-rate motel would run about seventy dollars, or seven times the cost of a pint of whiskey. Perhaps, like today's hotels in Las Vegas, Kinzie, Miller and Caldwell figured that once they got the people in, they would more than make up the cost of lodging in drink. One more striking thing is that it cost almost as much to feed and shelter a horse overnight as it did a human. But this was the world of Wolf Point "Chicago" in 1829.

In this world, there was no established government or law enforcement. Unlike the first settlements of the Pilgrims, there were no churches or community establishments to enforce what was still a social structure based on puritanical values. Thus, a typical scene at Wolf Point would serve as a precursor to many of today's alternative bars and dance clubs. Native Americans mixed with a few "Englishmen." Although it would be taboo in almost any other city in the settled eastern part of the United States, whites and Native Americans shared whiskey bottles and tobacco. Even more startling, Native American women and white women also "visited" these taverns, as races intermingled, drank and danced together. Less than a year after the tavern opened, in the spring of 1829, Billy Caldwell abandoned his wife for an Indian woman named "Josette." In June 1830, Caldwell was sued for divorce from his wife, Emily Hall Caldwell. Later that year, Hall married a discharged soldier.

Seeing economic opportunity, Mark Beaubien decided to open his own tavern, the Eagle Exchange, on the south bank of the river in 1829. A native of Detroit, he and his wife, Monique, moved to Chicago in 1826. For the first three years, they traded with the Indians. In 1829, they built a simple structure, the Eagle Exchange. Seeing that the tavern was on the opposite side of the river from the Wolf Tavern, Beaubien also decided to pitch in with another of Chicago's founders, Archibald Clybourn, to build a ferry that crossed the river. Between his duties tending the tavern and being on call in case somebody needed to use the ferry, Beaubien was a busy man. Yet his work ethic did not preclude Beaubien from having fun. A French Canadian Catholic and younger brother of Jean Baptiste Beaubien, Mark fit the pattern of the Acadian who traveled down the Mississippi River to Louisiana. Like the Cajuns, Beaubien loved to dance. He talked in a mixture of English and French. He played the fiddle. He loved food, drink and boasting. His best friend was Billy Caldwell, who was half Indian. In other words, Beaubien was a Chicago Cajun. His most famous quote was, "I plays de fiddle like de debble."

And he did. On countless warm summer nights under the moonlight, or in front of a blazing hot fireplace and stove, customers would call the tune and Beaubien's fiddle would be heard while settlers and Native Americans danced, passed jugs and smoked whatever tobacco could be found. The dancing often lasted until sunrise, as the chirping of the skylarks, loons, blackbirds and other river wildlife signaled that it was finally time for the

Wolf Point, home of Chicago's first business, the Wolf Point Tavern. *Wikimedia and Chicago Detours.*

party to end. Oftentimes, other French trappers would chime in on accordion and Native Americans on drums.

In 1831, Beaubien added an addition to the Eagle Exchange. A short time later, with the help of his wife, who had a keen eye for design, as well his brother, Colonel John Beaubien, the building was expanded even more. Built in a pioneer version of Greek Revival style, the structure was a great contrast to the simple cabins and structures that already existed at Wolf Point. In *Wau-Bun*, Juliette Kinzie described it as a "pretentious white two-story building, with bright blue wood shutters, the admiration of all the little circle at Wolf Point."

Beaubien decided to name the building the Sauganash Hotel. It was named after his good friend Billy Caldwell, a mixed descendant of a British officer and Potawatomi woman. Caldwell's Native American name was Sauganash, or "Englishman." Today, one of Chicago's most exclusive neighborhoods, nestled in the forest preserves on the far Northwest Side, is also named after him, as is the Billy Caldwell Golf Course. He also named the hotel in honor of his other Potawatomi friends who were forced to leave Chicago. Reportedly more than eight hundred braves performed their last war dance in front of the hotel.

Beaubien continued to entertain his guests with his fiddle. A drugstore was added next to the hotel. It was owned by a man named Philo Carpenter. Carpenter, however, was an early follower of what would come to be known as the temperance movement. A quarrel erupted between Beaubien and Carpenter over the excessive use of alcohol and the general rowdiness of the guests at the tavern. After a brief complaint, nothing changed, and a disgusted Carpenter left in haste.

Later that year, Beaubien ceded his management duties of the hotel. A booster of the city, Beaubien helped build Chicago's first Catholic church, served as light keeper on the Chicago River and a toll keeper in what is now DuPage County and opened another bar in Lisle, Illinois. In 1837, the building served as a full-time theater but quickly reopened as a hotel, lasting as such until it was burned down in 1851. A new structure, the Wigwam, was built on the same site in 1851. In 1860, the Republican National Convention was held at the Wigwam. Abraham Lincoln received the Republican nomination for president on land where, only thirty years earlier, nothing stood but cattails and ash trees. The site was designated as a Chicago Landmark on November 6, 2002.

In the meantime, Beaubien settled near Lisle. During the 1840s, he worked as a toll keeper on what was then called Southwest Plank Road and rented out space in his cabin to occasional travelers just to the west of what is now Lisle's Beaubien Cemetery. He returned to Chicago for a short time in 1859–60 to work as a lighthouse keeper on the Chicago River. But his memory and health were failing. Just as his great friend Billy Caldwell was a party to Chicago's first divorce, the years of drinking were taking its toll on Beaubien. In the spring of 1881, friends and family began to rally around him, including his son Frank, who left this entry in his diary: "Near the time of my father's death, just before he died he asked for his violin. He played an old Indian tune, the words are, 'Let me go to my home on the far distant shore white man, let me go.' He played it partly through, but he was too weak to finish."

Beaubien died from liver failure, or what is today called cirrhosis of the liver. While alcohol and distilled spirits provided much of Chicago's early growth and inspired many settlers, the damage that excessive use of alcohol can do to individuals and families must not be overlooked. (Both are covered in later chapters of this book on the temperance movement and "Skid Row.")

The last of Chicago's trio of first great taverns was the Green Tree Tavern. It was opened, once again, by James Kinzie at what is now the northeast corner of Chicago and Lake Streets in 1833. By this time, Elijah Wentworth was operating the Wolf Point Tavern, and Kinzie decided that there was also money to be made at the northwest corner of Wolf Point. Although stated in

The Green Tree Tavern, another of Chicago's first businesses. *Living History of Chicago.*

genteel terms, the Green Tree Inn still managed to have many of the rough-hewn qualities of its early predecessors Wolf Point and Sauganash.

After Chicago was incorporated as a city in 1837—it had been incorporated as a town four years earlier—more buildings and restaurants began to spring up along the muddy plank roads and soggy plots of land. By 1847, there were twenty-five hotels and taverns in Chicago. By this time, the pastimes of bowling and billiards, which had originated in Europe, were also becoming popular among the settlers. A precursor to the corner store, many establishments, then called "groceries," were opened. But while today's customers often purchase liquor from these establishments to bring back to their homes, these stores carried on the tradition of the Wolf Point Tavern. An article in the *Chicago Daily American* described the scene at and around these establishments:

> *The grocers or saloons dealing in liquor and groceries at the same time, were often the loafing places for a goodly number of ungentle rowdies, black-legs, sharpers, and other species of loafers, who indulged in drinking, swearing, fighting, and sometimes blocking the sidewalks during the evenings. Nor were they above operating the roulette wheel and gambling with cards.*

Beaubien's death was just one signal for what was to become the end of the early wild days of Wolf Point. In 1880, the Green Tree Tavern was loaded onto giant, soggy logs. With the help of a team of straining horses and mules and many sweating, swearing workers, the Green Tree was moved to what was then 33–37 Milwaukee Avenue between Fulton and Canal Streets.

Wolf Point Whiskey, a new distillery paying homage to the early days of whiskey. *Photo by author.*

Described as a "disjointed wreck of a building, with only a chimney atop," it survived for another fifty years. Its rotting and deteriorated state did not stop its inhabitants from imbibing inside though. Factory and tannery workers and meatpackers along Fulton Street had replaced the original pioneers as customers, but the two major draws—beer and whiskey—were the same.

In 1933, over a century after this makeshift structure of logs, mud and wood planks was hastily assembled, the Wolf Point Tavern was torn down. At the time it was built, a scant canoe, horse or man on foot could make his way through the wilderness among the site of wolves, Native American fires and trout, perch, beavers, herons and other wildlife living on the bounty of the river. One hundred years later, diesel engines, steamships and other boats crowded the river, trains and automobiles roared past and an occasional airplane flew overhead. Telephones had taken the place of letters carried on horseback. The building's final day was described in the August 18, 1933 edition of the *Chicago Tribune*:

> Built in 1830, another Chicago landmark, perhaps the oldest, has passed into the limbo of historical memories. It was wrecked to provide another loop area parking lot. Its rough-hewn timbers were reduced to a truck load of junk wood and kindling and hauled to a wrecking yard. Such was the end of a structure that had withstood the ravages of a century of progress. The building was an old tavern which stood at what is now 344 West Kinzie Street, near the north branch fork of the Chicago River. It is believed to have been built in about 1830 by Archibald Caldwell and James Klinale [sic] early Chicago settlers and was known as Wolf Point Tavern. Glimpses of its varied history were revealed yesterday by the Gries family, 8203 S. Wabash, present owners of the site. They said it was the only house of Kinzie Street that escaped the great Chicago Fire. In 1871, sailors and fisherman, they said, formed a bucket brigade and saved it, carrying water from the river and pouring it over the roof. Henry, 72 years old, who was superintendent of construction of the old World's Fair Fine Arts building, said he bought the old tavern in 1893 and operated it as a

saloon until prohibition. He said the walls, floors, and woodwork of the tavern were scarred by names, initials, and old Indian markings. Gries said that all the timber had been roughhewn, some of the planks being a foot thick and of a reddish mahogany color. No nails had been used in its construction, it was found when the wrecking firm of Anderson and Nelson tore it down last week.

Yet the old Wolf Point lives on. A new Chicago distillery, Wolf Point Distilling, is establishing itself in the old warehouse district, not far from the now developed Wolf Point. With a bottle that features a wolf standing in front of a campfire, its tradition harkens back to the first days of Chicagoland, when trappers, gathering to socialize after weeks in the wilderness, sat in front of campfires, listening to the wolves howl and most probably drinking whiskey.

THE WHISKEY TRUST

Whiskey Is Made Only in Peoria

Most of Chicago's streets are named after dead presidents, patriots and great leaders. But perhaps more than in any other major city, the monikers of many thoroughfares are named after men who made their fortunes brewing, barreling and bottling beer—not whiskey or spirits, which were made in Peoria. In fact, in 1880, Peoria produced more than 18 million gallons of alcohol. The entire state of Kentucky produced 15 million. But unlike Chicago's "Beer Baron Row," no fortunes were made off of distilling spirits in Chicago. No mansions were built, and no streets are named after prominent distillers. With plenty of fresh clean water, grain from barges and later railroads and plenty of thirsty men, it would seem that Chicago would have been an ideal place. The city got off to a rousing start producing alcohol, mainly in the form of beer.

William Ogden is remembered in Chicago, as Ogden Avenue is one of the major thoroughfares, running at a southwest angle from downtown through Chicago's neighborhoods and into adjoining suburbs like Lyons, Naperville and Downers Grove. A Chicago Public School is also named after him. Diversey Avenue is one of the North Side's major east–west thoroughfares, running from the shores of Lake Michigan west past the Chicago City limits on into Elmwood Park. Lill Avenue runs for a much shorter stretch, between Halsted and Racine, two blocks south of Diversey. Diversey and Lill represent two streets named after men who had a major impact on the city of Chicago. Both men made much of their fame and fortune brewing and selling beer. Names like Kinzie and Caldwell have already been mentioned. Going through a street or landmark guide to Chicago, you will find other names, like Conrad Sulzer, considered to be the founder of Lakeview and for whom the Sulzer Regional Library is named.

The first lager brewery in Chicago was the John A. Huck, or Huck and Schnieder Brewery, located near Wolcott and Division. Ogden also had an interest in the brewery. The brewery was opened in 1847, three years after the first true lager brewery was opened in Philadelphia. Other early breweries included the Matthias Best Brewery at Indiana and Lake Avenue, the Conrad Seipp Brewery at 27th Street and the lakeshore, the James Carney Brewery at 33–63 South Water Street, the Fortune Brothers Brewery at 138–144 Van Buren, the Mueller Brothers Brewery at 28 South Des Plaines, the Henry FL Rodmeyer Brewery at 378 Ohio Street, the Saberton Brewery and the Sibert and Schmidt Brewery. Later, the Schoenhofen Brewery at 18th and Canal was opened, and it eventually produced 100,000 gallons of beer per year. Many brewers in the late nineteenth century made small fortunes, building vast mansions in Wicker Park's "Beer Baron Row."

While the names of early brewers line Chicago's history, there are few distillers or distilleries of historical note. One reason is that unlike beer, especially lager beer, making corn liquor, applejack, rum and other spirits could be done relatively easily in a home or barn. Sure, the spirits were of poor quality, but almost every early settler had a friend or relative who made "hootch." This was also proven during Prohibition. There was an area on south Halsted, near the Union Stockyards, known as "Whiskey Row," but this was named as such more for the drunkards who inhabited it than actually whiskey being produced there.

Chicago's largest and best-known early distillery was Shufeldt and Company. Located at 54 South Water Street, Shufeldt opened in 1857. Homesteaders came to Shufeldt to buy alcohol for home needs such as kerosene lamps and stoves and other burning fluids. Alcohol was also used in manufacturing varnishes, perfumes, medicines, furniture polish and cleaners. There was also a small distillery. This changed with the arrival of a man named Thomas Lynch. Born in Ireland in 1826, he came to Chicago sometime around 1845. Apparently, whiskey making was his born trade, as he obtained work quickly working for a "rectifier" named Cosby. Rectifying is basically taking grain alcohol, neutral spirits and other forms of alcohol or non-bonded whiskey and mixing it with flavorings, colorings and syrups to produce a different form of booze. Peppermint schnapps is a perfect example of this type of concoction, as peppermint leaf (later fake peppermint flavoring) and sugary syrup are added to grain alcohol. Many of Chicago's early "distilleries," as well as the distributors that were run by organized crime almost until the twenty-first century, were actually rectifiers. Lynch was apparently very good at his job, for in a short time he took over the company, moving it to 128 North La Salle and changing the name to Thomas Lynch and Company. After relocating to Larrabee and Hawthorne Streets, he probably bought distilled alcohol from Shufeldt for his use in rectifying.

In 1871, the Great Chicago Fire changed everything. A curtain of flame starting south of downtown eventually enveloped much of the city. Fire spread from house to house as people jumped into the Chicago River. Panicked horses and livestock bolted through the city, eventually meeting cruel and painful deaths. Temperatures of more than five hundred degrees burned, melted and charred all but a few structures. Chicago's early distilleries, filled with extremely flammable grain and grain dust—as well as stores of pure alcohol, wooden bins and other flammable materials—burned with even greater fury. This was the first major blow to Chicago's distilleries. But the breweries—and many other businesses—reopened.

But not so for the distilleries. It was Peoria, Illinois, that became the whiskey capital of not just Illinois but the nation. *Peoria Magazine* reported that between 1837 and 1919, Peoria had seventy-three distilleries. The U.S. taxes derived from Peoria distillers were said to have paid off much of the national debt from the Civil War, and taxes from the Peoria tax collection district were estimated to have accounted for, in peak years, as much as half of the nation's annual tax revenue before the federal income tax bill was passed in 1913.

On the website Those Pro-Whiskey Men, author and blogger Jack Thompson noted:

> *My surmise is that in the wake of the fire, Lynch and Shufeldt joined forces in a distilling operation. The company kept the name Henry H. Shufeldt and Co. but Thomas Lynch was running the operation. The company built a new* [distilling] *facility near the Chicago Avenue Bridge and kept their offices and rectifying house at Kinzie and Cass Street. An illustration of the distillery claimed a capacity of 80,000 gallons. The company used the liquor stamp names of "Double Stamp," "Royal Arms" and "Imperial Gin." In 1878, at a Paris Exhibition, the distillery was awarded a gold medal for its whiskey.*

HIRAM WALKER AND SONS, INC. DISTILLERY, PEORIA, ILL.   4A-H1076

Hiram Walker Plant, Peoria, Illinois. *Author's collection.*

Like many of the men who made fortunes in brewing, Lynch used the money and prestige gained from the alcohol business to become a leading Chicago philanthropist and a prominent member of the Democratic Party, running unsuccessfully for Cook County treasurer in 1881. But changes were coming that would put an end to Chicago's distilling business for more than a century. These changes came in two forms: the Whiskey Trust and the city of Peoria. As Chicago's first great historian, Alfred T. Andreas, wrote, "Many of the distilleries have been closed by the Whiskey Trust which now owns them and finds that it is cheaper to make whiskey in…Peoria."

Established as a town in 1835 and a city in 1845, Peoria is also located on a major body of water, the Illinois River. The Illinois River flows downstream to the Mississippi River. During the 1880s, Peoria became a railroad hub. Unlike Chicago, Peoria is in the middle of the state, surrounded by some of the flattest, richest farmland in the world, as well as groves of white oak trees. It is also near some of the largest coal mines in the state. Thus, Peoria had easy and cheap access to grain to produce mash, limestone-filtered water to blend it with, coal to fire the stills and barrels to age it in. Once the liquor was made, these same rivers and railroads could transport the finished whiskey up the Illinois to Chicago and down the Mississippi to St. Louis, Memphis and New Orleans. This resulted in what many of America's leading bankers, distillers and businessmen saw as a perfect place to make whiskey. Thus, the

Advertisement for Old Crow Whiskey, circa 1870. *Library of Congress Historical Photo Collection.*

Whiskey Trust was born, and by the 1880s, Peoria had an estimated twenty-two distilleries.

Unlike beer, which spoils, whiskey is a commodity that can be stored, the price manipulated and then released on the market. It also needs to age. During this time of aging, small producers make no money. Bankers and other investors saw this as an opportunity to float loans to distillers so they had working capital during these periods. The banks would then collect the money once the whiskey was ready. These loans are referred to in the liquor industry as "warehouse receipts." Unlike the creation of organized crime, which can be traced directly to meetings between the likes of Lucky Luciano, Meyer Lansky and Frank Costello in upstate New York, history has not recorded the exact names, times and places where the Whiskey Trust or the Distillers and Cattle Feeders Trust began, but many historians point to a particular year, 1881, when Joseph Greenhut, Nelson Morris and John L. Francis built the Great Western Distillery.

Although there were distillers in Cincinnati, Chicago, New York and other cities, the bulk of the trustees deemed the trust be centered on Peoria. In Kentucky, many of the distillers were already established. Nevertheless, the Kentucky distillers like Makers Mark and Jim Beam were not part of the trust.

In his article "The Development of the Whiskey Trust," author Jerimiah Jenks stated, "At the time of the formation of the trust, it was thought by

Peoria's Clarke's Pure Rye Whiskey was a best-selling brand. *Randy Huetsch.*

some of the distillers living in Peoria that, on account of their unusual facilities for manufacturing, the trust should be limited to Peoria distilleries and a few others."

From 1883 to 1887, the trust continued. Much of the trust's work consisted of regulating the price of whiskey. When the first meeting was held in 1881, higher taxes on whiskey as well as corn had many distillers operating at a loss. In order to change this, the trust began to manipulate the price of whiskey. The owners did this by lowering production at the facilities they controlled, paying the smaller distributors not to produce whiskey or simply buying out the smaller distributorships and shutting them down. This should have been the case with Chicago's Shufeldt & Company, but Lynch had other ideas. Lynch was reported to have stated, "How such an organization as the 'Trust' is allowed to exist, I cannot understand. It has issued $35,000,000 of certificates and I can prove that it is not in possession of more than $4,000,000 worth of property." To which a legal representative for the trust replied, "The Trust might easily put up these prices of spirits but it cannot do so as long as Shufeldt holds out and it would be a mighty good thing for the Trust if Shufeldt is out of the way."

In his 1889 article, Jenks continued, "The most formidable rivals of the trust, Shufeldt & Co. of Chicago, who had doubtless also made large gains from the increase in price and who had run their distillery at even more of the normal capacity…are even building a new house of 3000 bushels capacity."

Something had to be done. First, it was reported that employees of the Whiskey Trust were working as spies. In September 1888, it was also reported that valves, vats and other mechanical processes of the distillery had been tampered with, another form of industrial espionage, or that a chemical accident may have caused an explosion. But in what may have been a precursor to Chicago's days of bootlegging and mayhem, on December 11, 1888, a man or group of men still unidentified today walked down Chicago's cold streets. It was still dark, and many of the busy horse and buggy livery wagons, peddlers, pushcart men and businessmen in their top hats and stick-pinned collars had yet to enter the area. Perhaps a few straggling men living in or lining the area stood around a smoldering coal barrel fire, but this was doubtful in this industrial part of the city. A fuse was set, and into the cold, dark sky two bundles of dynamite, each containing seven sticks, sailed through the air and onto the roof of Shufeldt's storeroom. Witnesses report that at about 6:15 a.m., a tremendous explosion thundered through the area. Not just the small wooden outhouses and shacks but even large buildings shook. Horses whinnied. The sheer force of the dynamite was said to have shattered windows for blocks, sending shards of glass tumbling onto the brick- and wood-paved alleys and streets. Apparently, only one of the bombs exploded, but it was enough to do considerable damage.

In his book *Sketches of the North American United States*, author Peter A. Demens wrote, "Several weeks ago, the Illinois whiskey trust's hired agents dynamited a distillery in Chicago that refused to enter the combine."

The trust, of course, denied the incident, and while a man named Gibson was charged with sabotage, nothing came of the charges. In another, rather telling, precursor to the days of Al Capone, shortly after the explosion, Lynch changed his mind and sold his shares to the trust. He did so, however, at a reported profit of more than $1 million. Lynch said that he was selling his shares not to the trust, but to the First National Bank of Chicago and in particular a man named Thomas Gage, who was later to become secretary of the treasury under President McKinley. Following in the footsteps of Wacker and others, Lynch's sons used the money made from the distillery sale to become prominent Chicago businessmen. John Lynch became president of Chicago's National Bank of the Republic, and James Lynch became president of the Globe Automatic Telephone Company.

Thompson wrote, "Nevertheless, it was the trust that ran H.H. Shufeldt Co. from 1881 on. They closed the Chicago distilling and rectifying operation and moved equipment to Pekin, Il. An office for the firm continued to be listed in Chicago business directories until 1917."

Although there were many rectifiers that bottled, labeled and distributed spirits, the dynamiting of Shufeldt marked the end of any major, legal grain to tube to barrel distilling in Chicago for more than a century.

In Peoria, however, the whiskey business raged on. In 1843, Almiran S. Cole launched the first distillery in the town. But since he didn't know much about whiskey making, the enterprise soon folded. However, in 1850, Cole enlisted the help of Tobias Bradley, William Moss and Benjamin Bourland, and soon he was turning a profit. But it did not stop there. During the 1860s and 1870s, the number of distilleries doubled, creating a "distillery row" along the Illinois River from State Street to the I-174 bridge. Around 1881, the Whiskey Trust set up shop in Peoria. In 1881, Joseph Greenhut

Whiskey distillery, circa 1915. *Library of Congress Historical Photo Collection.*

opened the Great Western Distillery, and by the end of the decade, Peoria had twelve distilleries, with four more in nearby Pekin and Canton. Bernie Drake, a former president of the Peoria Historical Society, stated, "Peoria remained its headquarters, with Peoria distilleries accounting for 50 percent of the trust's production. By 1890, the trust was operating only six distilleries in Peoria—so those six Peoria distilleries accounted for 50 percent of the nation's total trust production and 40 percent of all alcohol produced in the United States."

In all, Peoria was said to have hosted twenty-three breweries and seventy-three distilleries between 1847 and 1919. The website Straight Bourbon stated that in 1893, 185,000 gallons were being produced every twenty-four hours and 18.6 million gallons of alcohol per year. The corn by-product, mash, was said to have fed as many as twenty-eight thousand animals.

Uncle Sam took notice. After the Civil War, the whiskey tax stamp was the major source of revenue for the U.S. Treasury, and it is said that monies gained from whiskey helped to pay off the Civil War debt. In 1894, some estimate that the United States received 42 percent of its revenue from liquor taxes.

In 1893, the Whiskey Trust was on its way to being disbanded. Clarke Brothers, which was once part of the trust, became Peoria's best-known distiller. It billed itself as "The Largest Distillery in the World," primarily through its sale of Clarke Brothers Pure Rye. The brand's symbol was an older, stern, Yankee-faced man who was known as "the Old Codger." Just as "The Dude," played by Jeff Bridges in *The Big Lebowski* a century later, symbolizes a kind of quiet, inebriated rebellion, Clarke's "Old Codger" was his direct predecessor. Portrayed on everything from labels on bottles to mirrors, signs and even the joker on a deck of playing cards, the "old dude" helped make Peoria's Clarke Brothers Pure Rye a top-selling national brand.

Yet as time went on, many of the original trust members, who began in the 1880s, were aging or had died. Expanded rail and even some early trucking operations helped decentralize the making of spirits. The Whiskey Trust was already in decline, but Prohibition largely put an end to Peoria's era as the "Whiskey Capital of the World."

In 1933, Hiram Walker, a Canadian company, opened a huge plant on the city's riverfront—on the site of the Great Western Distillery, the operation once owned by Joseph Greenhut, the tycoon who formed the infamous Whiskey Trust. Clarke Brothers was bought by U.S. Industrial Alcohol Inc. and its Pure Rye label was purchased by Arrow Distilleries Inc., but the brand disappeared altogether in 1943.

Today, there are few remnants of Peoria's Whiskey Row. Phil Luciano, a writer for the *Peoria Journal Star*, noted, "Archer Daniels Midland now occupies the last working remnant of a distillery, Hiram Walker. And many mansions, which still stand on High Street, were built by whiskey barons."

THE TEMPERANCE MOVEMENT

Anchored in Chicago

*Drunkenness is the source of domestic misery and of poverty and wretchedness
so degrading that God alone can measure the curse.*
—Marie Brehm, Woman's Christian Temperance Union

It may have been an ocean and half a continent away, but by the 1880s, Chicago still had more than a few elements of Charles Dickens's London. While prosperous brewers and businessmen were building mansions on Prairie Avenue, laborers toiled across the city, many of them in the "standard" conditions for workers of the time. In the Union Stockyards, named after the American "union," men toiled in one-hundred-degree heat or freezing temperatures, axe, knife and sledgehammer in hand, knee-deep in blood, intestines and brain matter. They spent their days killing, cutting and slicing amid the stench of rotting flesh, over the sound of animals squealing and baying at the pain and sight of their imminent slaughter. Mills and factories, having sprung up after the Great Fire, had men working in twelve-hour shifts in dark, smoky buildings often with no windows or ventilation. The noise was deafening. Machines malfunctioned. Fingers, hands and even limbs were injured or sometimes severed, with no "workman's comp," save passing the hat. Many returned home to shacks and overcrowded buildings with no running water or outdoor toilets, chickens and livestock roaming the streets and a sewage system that, before the reversal of the Chicago River, left dysentery and disease in certain areas.

One escape from this environment was alcohol. Men flocked to the corner tavern before work, after work and between shifts and took buckets of beer and flasks of whiskey with them to their homes. Today, even with science, treatment and modern social and medical services, alcoholism is a problem that affects millions of Americans. One can only imagine its impact in the middle of the nineteenth century. This was especially true in Chicago, where beer and whiskey were cheap, easily available and consumed in massive quantities. In 1865, it was estimated that the average Chicago household consumed three gallons of beer per week. By 1900, it was sixteen gallons. Add to that the massive amounts of whiskey, rum, gin, wine and other ethnic and homemade alcoholic concoctions. In many cases, the results were devastating. Drunken men stumbled through the streets, eventually passing out or sleeping in alleys, gutters, gangways and yards. Alcohol fueled countless brawls, as men emerged from bars with bloodied faces, busted noses, broken limbs and even stab wounds and fatal injuries. During the summer heat, oftentimes with no supply of fresh, cold water, men "cooled off" with more beer. Today, we know that alcohol actually dehydrates, but during that era they did not, and the result was men drinking more and more beer and ale, eventually wandering the streets sweating, panting, limbs shaking and sometimes even dying. During the

Temperance ladies protest. *Library of Congress Historical Photo Collection.*

winter, there were no "warming centers," and those same alleys and gangways were filled with a different group of men, overcome by liquor, passed out and frozen stiff. They were often picked up like cords of wood by horse-drawn police wagons making the rounds.

If these intoxicated workers did make it back to the "safety" of home, the results were often no better. At best, paychecks were wasted on liquor and bills; food and clothing for the children were neglected. At worst, physical, sexual and emotional abuse by some drunken husbands on their spouses and children would be astounding by today's standards.

The solution to these problems lay in temperance, brought about by the hand of God. Across the nation, the message of the temperance movement was spreading. Crusaders distributed songs, sermons and literature across the city, as evidenced by the popular songs/sermons like "The Drink That Is in the Drunkard's Bowl," published in the *Chicago Daily American*:

The drink that's in the drunkard's bowl, is not the drink for me;
It kills the body and the soul; How sad a sight is he!
But there's a drink which God has given, distilling in the showers of heaven,
In measures large and free, O that's the drink for me.
The stream that many prize so high, Is not the stream for me;
For he that drinks it still is dry, Forever dry he'll be.
But there's a stream for me; For he who drinks it, still is dry, forever dry
he'll be.
But there's a stream so cool and clear,
The thirsty traveler lingers near,
Refreshed and glad is he; O that's the stream for me.

The wine cup that so many prize, Is not the cup for me;
The aching head and bloated face, In its' sad train I see.
But there's a cup of water pure, and he who drinks it may be sure
Of health and length of days; O' that's the cup for me.

Chicago's temperance movement began in 1833, not long after Kinzie, Beaubien, Miller and the city fathers began operating the Wolf Point, Green Tree and Eagle Exchange Taverns. It was that year that the Chicago Temperance Society was founded with an estimated 120 members. Members campaigned throughout the city as well as in Fort Dearborn before it was officially decommissioned in 1837. Ironically, the forces of alcohol and whiskey traders had triumphed over those who wanted to end the whiskey trade twenty-five years earlier. The early message of temperance apparently fared a bit better, as the diary of Charles Butler reported that forty men had joined the movement, "elevating the standard character of the army."

In 1842, at a meeting of Chicago's first and oldest church, the First United Methodist Church, the Chicago Washington Temperance Society established a constitution. Later that year, it combined forces with the Chicago Catholic Temperance Society, organizing a march through the city complete with banners and printed pamphlets.

By 1847, Chicago had two Washington Temperance Societies, three tents of the Independent Order of Rechabites, three divisions of the Sons of Temperance, the Chicago Bethel (Seaman's) Temperance Society and the Catholic Benevolent Temperance Society branch of the American Temperance Society. These organizations set up lodges, as well as temperance boardinghouses, and held tent revivals and lectures throughout the city. They helped fuel the mighty but temporarily failed laws to close saloons on Sunday, which resulted in the Lager Beer Riots. This event, which occurred in 1855, is still known as Chicago's first major civil disturbance. The early prohibitionists, led by Mayor Levi Boone, proposed and passed a bill to close saloons and drinking establishments such as beer gardens on Sundays. For Chicago's Germanic immigrants, Sunday was always a day off, meant to spend outdoors or in a saloon. News of the bill filtered through the North Side neighborhoods, including what is now Old Town. Men with pitchforks, shotguns, pistols and other blunt instruments marched downtown and surrounded city hall. As news spread, more came. In a state of shock, it was ordered that the bridges over the Chicago River be raised to stop the swarms of rioters from entering downtown, a method that was used again in 2020 during the Black Lives Matter civil disturbances. Literally surrounded, Mayor Boone had no choice but to squash the law. But some of the groundwork for temperance had already been laid. A bill to pass the liability to saloon keepers for damages done through overserving of alcohol passed in Maine in 1851. Known as the Dram Shop Act, similar legislation, drafted by Abraham Lincoln, passed both branches of the Illinois General Assembly. But the populace defeated the bill in a referendum in 1855.

Ellen Stone, a driving force in the temperance movement. *Library of Congress Historical Photo Collection.*

But the largest, most powerful, lasting and important temperance organization in Chicago and the Chicago area was the Woman's Christian Temperance Union (WCTU). Its first major event took place on the evening of March 16, 1874. Fifty-seven women marched from the Clark Street Methodist Episcopal Church, where they had gathered a church full of protesters, to the city council chambers, four blocks away. They met at the downtown church to protest the Chicago city council's attempt to modify the city's saloon law and allow saloons to open for business on Sundays. Armed with a petition with sixteen thousand signatures favoring defeat of the proposed ordinance, the women were determined that the opposition be heard by the city council. After some debate, the councilmen agreed to listen to the protesters and have the petition presented, and then they quickly voted to pass the ordinance, deliberately thwarting the women's goals.

For the women, the most revealing and perhaps mobilizing part of the experience occurred after the council rejected their petition. A writer for the *Chicago Herald* reported, "While they had been waiting, the rabble began to gather on the outside, blocking all avenue of approach. Adams Street had been blocked by perhaps the most ruffianly crowd ever assembled in the city—a crowd gathered to insult anyone bearing the semblance of a lady. It had been gathered from the saloons and slums to give the bummer alderman moral support. Accordingly, every saloon had stood threat to the deadbeats who would ordinarily be ordered out of the place on the condition they would make 'Rome howl.' When the woman left the chamber, they had to pass through a gauntlet of a shouting and hooting mob, during which the obscenest epithets were bandied about, the foulest epithets applied."

Many credited the organized opposition to Eighth Ward alderman James H. Hildreth. But no matter who organized it, hindsight revealed that this may have been the wrong approach. For these women, tempered by the tragedy of the Great Chicago Fire just three years before and the Civil War a decade earlier, were now given a resolve and mettle that was to temporarily change the course of local Chicago politics. Their mission began shortly after the city hall slander, as groups of women began to enter saloons and pray and sing until the embarrassed patrons left. Women also brought platters to the bars, stating, "Presumed husband you were too busy to come home, so I brought dinner here." But when the men lifted the platter, it bore only a note stating, "Men are wanted in the church and in Christian homes. Help! Help! The master calls your loved one's home."

In 1874, the headquarters of the organization was located in the Bethel Home at Lake and Des Plaines Streets. At the time, it was a small organization led by Annie Wittenmeyer. However, a movement was growing, and like most movements, it needed a leader. This leader turned out to be Frances Willard. Willard was becoming a leading national figure in not only the WCTU, where she served as president from 1879 until her death in 1898, but also the women's movement and other reforms. In some ways, Willard has been compared with Jane Addams and Lucy Parsons, two Chicagoans who became leaders of the early women's movement and influenced social issues.

"Frances Willard was a former teacher and Dean of the Woman's College at Northwestern," said Janet Olsen, archivist at the Willard House and Museum in Evanston, Illinois. "In 1874 she attended the founding convention of The Woman's Christian Temperance Union and became the Secretary and in 1876 became President of the Chicago branch of the WCTU."

Willard was also the director of publications for the organization. The 1876 WCTU report, issued in September, stated, "A growing cancer positions the blood of the body politic. We have protected with all the insignia of law the demon which continually transforms plenty into poverty, happiness into horror, genius into imbecility, and hope to despair. There will be no peace in the home while the saloon stands."

A short time later, however, Willard resigned her office and quit her jobs as secretary and Chicago president largely due to a dispute with then current president Annie Wittenmeyer. Wittenmeyer, it seemed, did not want to link the issues of women's suffrage and temperance, saying in effect that politics was not a place for women, but a safe home was. Willard saw them as being linked, stating that "the object of which is to secure for all women above the age of twenty-one years the ballot as one means for the protection of their homes from the devastation caused by the legalized traffic in strong drink."

Willard continued her opposition to Wittenmeyer, and in 1879, Willard's opinion seemed to hold sway, as she was elected president of the WCTU. "Willard's vision was huge," Olsen said. "She saw an opportunity to end alcoholism and empower women, linking home protection with the right to vote."

The women of America, it seemed, agreed. In 1881, just after Willard took office, the WCTU had a national membership of 22,800.

MISS FRANCES E. WILLARD.

Frances Willard, longtime head of the WCTU. *Author's collection.*

The home of Frances Willard in Evanston, Illinois, now a museum and learning center. *Photo by author.*

By 1891, it had swelled to 138,377. Much of the WCTU's business had previously been conducted in Willard's home in Evanston, Illinois. In fact, the home is now a museum and landmark dedicated to Willard's life and career fighting for temperance and other women's issues. This led to major innovations within the organization, which included Chicago. The WCTU Chicago headquarters had been located at the Republic Life Building in a small office space. But as the membership grew, so did their needs. Willard was not only a great writer, organizer and leader but a businesswoman as well. As she began her term, she was lobbying city leaders like Marshall Field. Plans were announced, and in 1892, a magnificent National Headquarters for the Woman's Christian Temperance Union was built on the corners of Monroe and La Salle Streets. "The building was called the Woman's Temple and it was planned and built in time to be a significant structure, representing the WCTU when the World's Fair came to Chicago in 1893," Olsen said.

The building, which cost $1,500,000, was a showcase and evidence of the influence of the temperance movement and the WCTU in Chicago. Designed by John Root of Burnham and Root, it was twelve stories high with three hundred offices and seven passenger elevators capable of carrying fifteen thousand passengers per day. The ground floor contained four banks: the National Bank of America, the Bank of Commerce, the Metropolitan National Bank and the Bank of Montreal. The following description was taken by the Rand McNally *Bird's Eye Views and Guide to Chicago*:

> *The entrance is from Monroe Street. This beautiful room, in which symbolical fountains of water play, is lighted by windows commemorating temperance workers, and is ceiled* [sic], *wainscoted, and walled with marble tablets, recording the names of those who put money in this edifice. Commercial interests and the necessity of immediate profit modified somewhat the original plans of the Temperance Union. More business gradually forced its way into the enterprise, until, instead of the Woman's Christian Temperance Temple, it is the Woman's Temple, with an option in contract whereby, for so many years, the property is open to redemption by the Union itself, in which event it may call it what it pleases and use it as the Union sees fit. There will naturally gather in the Woman's Temple a high class of tenants. Sculptors, architects, and painters, men of genius generally, will find many encouragements where the atmosphere is so largely one of public spirit. Carl Kohl-Smith, the Danish sculptor who designed the statue of Franklin at the Electricity Building in Jackson Park, was one of the first to establish himself here. The building, of course, presents all the marvels of modern domestic construction. White marble, black iron, shining brass, green onyx, red tiling, and yellow oak combine to gratify the eye with color. Modern plumbing, mail-chutes, electric calls, gas and Edison lights, equable warmth, ventilators, hot and cold water, café and many hundred fellow-tenants, whereby a city life and correspondence may be established within the building.*

Ironically, the description stated "men of genius" and did not mention women. Legend also has it that at the opening ceremony, Root stated, "Now that it is done, let's go have a drink." Nevertheless, it gave the WCTU a major presence nationally, anchored in Chicago. But that was not the last vision or change that Willard would impart on the temperance movement.

"Willard was far ahead of her time in so many ways," Olsen noted. "She worked to include both women and children in the movement, educating children on the evils of alcohol, not only the moral evils, but the physical evils. These lessons were first taught in Sunday school, but she also began to include scientific findings which eventually led to temperance and the dangers of alcohol being taught as part of the 'health' curriculum in schools.

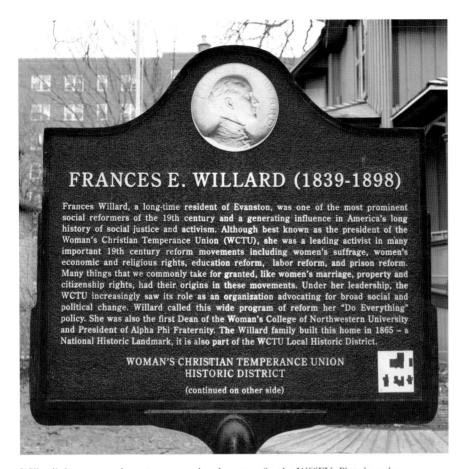

Willard's home served as a temporary headquarters for the WCTU. *Photo by author.*

Willard also began to secularize Temperance." Olsen continued, "She saw that taking only the moral path did not bear weight with many 'drunks,' so she not only applied God's work through Christianity, that drinking would send you to hell, but also that drinking will destroy your health. In this way she had a much stronger argument."

Willard also campaigned against the many traveling "elixir salesmen" of the era. Dressed in ornate suits, top hats and fancy ties, they often, like the "wizard" from L. Frank Baum's *Wizard of Oz*, traveled in covered wagons with plaques proclaiming doctoral degrees and selling bottled "cures" for alcoholism. "She worked to discredit these men, like Leslie E. Keeley from Dwight, Illinois, who said he devised a drink containing gold, and if you drank the tincture it would cure alcoholism," Olsen noted.

Willard died in 1897. The WCTU headquarters was demolished in 1926, one of many great architectural marvels lost in Chicago. Besides the Willard House, Museum and Archives in Evanston, another lasting "monument" to the WCTU is the "Fountain Girl." The "Fountain Girl" was the best known of many "Temperance Fountains." As stated before, there were no soft drinks and water was often impure. The WCTU decided to provide fresh, cool water to potential drinkers from the fountains. Originally called "The Little Cold Water Girl," it was placed at the 1893 World's Fair primarily to dissuade men from patronizing the numerous beer tents that mushroomed along the Midway. After the fair, the fountain was moved to the new WCTU Temple and Headquarters. Bearing a striking resemblance to Savannah, Georgia's *Bird Girl*—the Sylvia Shaw Judson sculpture made famous by the book and subsequent movie *Midnight in the Garden of Good and Evil*—the fountain became a city attraction. It also spurred on a movement across the city to erect water and drinking fountains in neighborhoods as well as in parks and public buildings. The purpose was twofold. It promoted health and provided clear, cold water as an alternative to alcoholic beverages. The fountain was moved to Lincoln Park in 1921. After being moved east of the La Salle Street underpass near North Avenue in 1940, the statue was stolen in 1958. The four-and-a-half-foot figure was recast and rededicated just east of the Chicago History Museum in 2013.

In 1877, while Willard and Wittenmeyer were struggling over the leadership of the WCTU, the Pacific Garden Mission was formed. Today, it stands as the oldest organization of its kind in the nation. Its first building was at 386 South Clark Street. The Mission moved to 67 East Van Buren in 1880. In 1923, it moved to 646 South State Street, within shouting distance of Chicago's infamous Levee District. Today, it stands at 1458 South Canal, just north of the old Schoenhofen Brewery.

While some Chicagoans still remember the horrors of Chicago's infamous Skid Row, which ran along West Madison Street until the 1980s, it is hard to imagine the devastation of the human spirit that Clark and his wife, Sarah, must have faced when they opened the mission's doors in 1880. At that time, there was little or no care or "safety net" whatsoever for the poor. Men struggling with alcoholism wandered the streets, dazed with unshaven, pockmarked faces from the elements, beatings, vermin and filth. Besides dehydration, withdrawal "shakes" and other alcohol-related symptoms, diseases like tuberculosis, rheumatic fever and viruses of all kinds spread unchecked through coughing, sneezing, vomiting, rodents

The "Fountain Girl," a WCTU fountain, was placed downtown to promote the drinking of clean water instead of alcohol. *Photo by author.*

and feces of men who lived on the streets or in crowded shacks made of bits of wood and tin lined with rags.

During the winter, conditions were even worse. The shacks and small fires made in tin pots from scraps were of little help in defense against Chicago's constant snow, subfreezing temperatures and howling winds. Most had coats, but gloves and socks usually consisted of tattered, often blood-soaked, filthy rags. Food consisted of rotted pieces of meat, and men fought with dogs and rats for morsels tossed in the alleys, as during that time the streets had no regular garbage collection.

These sights moved first Sarah Dunn Clarke and later her husband, George. The following on how the mission was formed is taken from a written sermon from Dan Graves, MSL, from *Modern Christianity Magazine* and later its website:

> *She persuaded her husband (who had become a Christian) to visit the city slums, with their gambling halls, saloons, and brothels. He went but was more interested in making money than dealing with human wrecks. However, while he was on a business trip a thousand miles away, he felt the Lord Jesus stab him with sharp conviction that people matter more than money. He dropped to his knees and consecrated himself to God's service. Immediately he telegraphed his wife of his change of plans.*

Upon his return to Chicago, George Clarke began to preach to the broken men and women of Chicago's slums, although his friends considered him one of the world's worst preachers. And yet through his love and concern, lives were changed.

On September 15, 1877, Colonel George and Sarah Clarke opened a mission on South Clark Street. In a space that once housed a tiny store, they set up wooden benches to seat forty people. As the colonel wept and struggled to speak words that would change hearts, Sarah did her best to keep order among the noisy and drunken people who came in. The Clarkes saw it as a work of the Holy Spirit, where many lives were changed.

Five years later, the mission moved to a bigger building that had been the Pacific Beer Garden. Dwight L. Moody suggested its new name. "Strike out the 'beer' and add 'mission,'" he suggested. And so the Pacific Garden Mission got its name.

As in many missions, men were given a meal, a bed and sometimes clothing in exchange for listening to sermons that derided the evils of alcohol. Oftentimes, longtime residents had to pledge an oath of sobriety in order

The Pacific Garden Mission, established in 1877, was part of the early efforts to end the alcoholism of Skid Row. *Photo by author.*

to continue to receive services. But upon seeing the devastation and poverty that the men of the streets of that era faced, the call of God was a strong tonic for many. Evangelist Dwight L. Moody, who started the Moody Bible Church, which is today one of Chicago's largest churches, began his career at the Pacific Garden Mission. So too did the man whom many consider to be the most famous and popular pro-temperance speaker of the late nineteenth and early twentieth centuries, Reverend Billy Sunday. Sunday was a professional baseball player who played for the Chicago White Stockings (forerunner to the Chicago Cubs, not the White Sox), and his influence was so great that many say that he was the most famous preacher in American history besides Billy Graham. The character played by Burt Lancaster in the film *Elmer Gantry*, taken from Sinclair Lewis's book, was partially modeled after Sunday. He was immortalized further by songwriter Fred Fisher. His song "Chicago," made famous by Frank Sinatra, referred to Sunday and the temperance movement in the lyrics "the town that Billy Sunday could not shut down."

"I never saw my father," Sunday wrote in his autobiography. A Union soldier, his father joined Iowa's 23rd Volunteer Infantry in 1862 and died of pneumonia in a Confederate prison camp four months later. Just a few weeks before, he had received a later that his son Billy was born. Things did not get any easier for Billy. His mother could not support the family, and at ten, Sunday was placed in an orphanage in Davenport, Iowa. Here, his life began to take on some semblance of structure, and Sunday was by all accounts a well-liked and happy young man. Like Babe Ruth, another famous orphan who also dominated the 1920s, Sunday was noticed for his speed and athleticism and soon began playing baseball on club teams around Marshalltown, Iowa.

There he was noticed by two of the seminal figures in early baseball history, Adrian "Cap" Anson and A.G. Spalding, whose name is still on millions of baseballs in major-league and other parks around the world. At that time, he was president of the White Stockings, and at Anson's behest, Sunday was signed to a major-league contract in 1883.

His speed and the excitement he created made him a hit with the fans, and he was also well-liked by his teammates. One day in 1887, Sunday and his

White Stocking teammates were enjoying an afternoon on South Wabash Avenue, not far from what was then the Levee District. But that afternoon, Sunday did not fit in. He wrote, "I never drank much. I was never drunk but four times in my life.…I used to go to the saloons with the baseball players, and while they would drink highballs gin and beer, I would take lemonade."

Instead, he heard strains of a sermon at the Pacific Garden Mission a block away on South State Street. Perhaps it was like a vision in a movie, where clouds parted and rays of sun broke through the hot Chicago sky. More likely, it was his life rushing before him. Looking at the men standing inside the mission, with their tattered clothes, unkempt hair, shaggy beards and red, pockmarked skin sweating in the hot sun, he may have recalled his impoverished early childhood. Then the music, the preacher and the missionaries, dressed in their uniforms, and the orderly procession may have represented his salvation—the structure and order of the orphanage. Whatever the cause, Sunday was overcome with emotion. A short time later, he became a Christian and regularly attended the Jefferson Park Presbyterian Church. He soon married Helen "Nell" Thompson, the daughter of a prosperous dairy merchant. In 1888, he was traded to the Pittsburgh Alleghenys. Although he continued to thrill fans with his stolen bases, his weak hitting became even weaker. Perhaps in an effort to make "spectacular" plays, Sunday began to make "spectacular" errors. Maybe his skills were deteriorating or maybe he was overcome by his calling, but as author Lisle Dorsett wrote, "In the spring of 1891, Sunday turned down a baseball contract for $3,500 a year to accept a position with the Chicago YMCA at $83 per month. Sunday's job title at the YMCA was Assistant Secretary, yet the position involved a great deal of ministerial work. It proved to be good preparation for his later evangelistic career. For three years Sunday visited the sick, prayed with the troubled, counseled the suicidal, and visited saloons to invite patrons to evangelistic meetings."

Sunday then went on the road with evangelist J. Wilbur Chapman. It was here that he learned the life of traveling dusty roads, erecting tents and lighting kerosene lamps, but most importantly, he learned the power of presenting a well-dressed clean-cut figure who preached the gospel of the Lord to the often poor, unsophisticated and uneducated townspeople of rural America. In 1896, Sunday went out on his own. His career as a baseball player helped draw large crowds, and his reputation and audiences grew. Soon, tents turned into wooden structures, and donations of quarters, nickels and dimes grew into dollars, which soon turned into a tidy personal fortune. In a time before modern media, news of his arrival

Billy Sunday leaving the White House. He was the spiritual advisor to the White House from 1921 to 1932. *Library of Congress Historical Photo Collection.*

spread by word of mouth, crude signs nailed to trees and an almost electric excitement that ran through the towns he visited. Estimates vary, but most agree that the number of people he preached to was in the millions—and for good reason. Before amplification, Sunday spoke in a high-pitched voice that bore a slight resemblance to Franklin D. Roosevelt. But it was his stage antics that wowed the crowds. Sunday was a tornado of energy. Using the entire stage, he would wave his arms, stomp, cajole, take off his white suit coat and toss it on the ground or wade into the audience, which he often brought to seizures, fits of shaking or cascades of tears. His message may have concerned sin in the broadest terms, but foremost it was liquor. In a period when the temperance movement was at its height, he would send his booming message across the urban streets of Chicago or the farm fields of the nation. The following are excerpts from his most famous speech, the "Booze" speech in Boston:

> *I am the sworn, eternal and uncompromising enemy of the liquor traffic. I have been, and will go on, fighting that damnable, dirty, rotten business with all the power at my command. I shall ask no quarter from that gang, and they shall get none from me.…*
>
> *Listen! Seventy-five per cent of our idiots come from intemperate parents, 80 per cent of the paupers, 82 per cent of the crime is committed by men under the influence of liquor, 90 per cent of the adult criminals are whiskey made. The Chicago Tribune kept track for 10-years and found that 53,438 murders were committed in the saloons.*
>
> *Look at Kansas. It is dry. In 85 of 105 counties in Kansas there is not one idiot. In 38 counties they have not a single pauper in the poorhouse, and there are only 600 dependents in the whole State. In 65 counties in Kansas they did not have a single prisoner in the county jails in the year 1912, and in some of the counties the grand jury hasn't been called to try a criminal case in 10 years.…The Legislature of Illinois appropriated $6,000,000 in 1908 to take care of the insane people in the state, and the whiskey business produces 75 per cent of the insane. Who gets the money? The saloon keepers and the brewers, and the distillers, while the whiskey fills the land with misery, poverty, wretchedness, disease, death, and damnation!*

During a career that lasted almost forty years, Sunday became not only a celebrity but also an important figure in politics, as Woodrow Wilson, Theodore Roosevelt and Herbert Hoover were counted as his friends. He also made as much as $900 per day at a time when the average worker made that in a year. During Sunday's peak of popularity, other temperance groups, including the Anti-Saloon League, also rose in political and economic power.

Sunday died on November 6, 1935, in Chicago. He is buried at Forest Lawn Cemetery in Forest Park, Illinois, just outside the city limits. His

Billy Sunday's grave, located just outside Chicago in Forest Park, Illinois. *Photo by author.*

goal, and the goal of the WCTU, was successful, since in 1919 the Eighteenth Amendment to the Constitution was passed. The Volstead Act also passed, giving the amendment the power of law enforcement to back it up. Sunday's speeches and causes helped to eventually enact Prohibition, but if you listen to his "Booze" sermon closely, portions of it centered on whiskey, money, the U.S. Treasury and taxes. Much of what he spoke about did not actually take place in Chicago, but Peoria, Illinois. It was here where another temperance leader, Carrie Nation, arrived in 1901. In what might be her most famous picture, she took an axe to the distilleries of this Illinois river town, rallying against what was then the whiskey capital of the United States. Although still twenty years away, the temperance movement was well on its way to changing the face of America.

CHICAGO'S IMMIGRANT POPULATION, THE LEVEE AND THE COMING OF PROHIBITION

By the late nineteenth and twenties centuries, Chicago had changed from a city composed of early settlers and German/Irish immigrants to a tapestry of tastes, languages and cultures. Immigrants from Poland, Italy, Serbia, Greece, Bohemia/Czechoslovakia, Lithuania, Sweden, Norway and other, mainly European nations arrived in Chicago by the hundreds of thousands. It was before the eight-hour day, and whether it was in a factory, toiling amid belching smoke, searing flames and the near deafening sound of machinery; building houses largely by hand in the wind, sun, snow and rain; or standing knee-deep in blood and guts, knife in hand, carving carcasses over the dying cries of livestock in the stockyards like Jurgis Rudkus in Upton Sinclair's *The Jungle*, work in the late nineteenth and early twentieth centuries was nothing like we know it today. Much to the dismay of those fighting for the ongoing temperance movement, these immigrants brought with them social traditions that relied even more heavily on the consumption of alcohol. As a great many of these immigrants worked in factories, lived in tenement housing and suffered much discrimination, the reliance on alcohol only increased. Speaking in general terms, it can be said that a majority of Chicago's new immigrant cultures enjoyed beer and spirits as a semi-regular part of their social interaction. While the type of beer was generally local lagers, these ethnic groups enjoyed an extremely diverse array of distilled spirits.

For the Germans, it began with German food such as wiener schnitzel and bratwurst. Food and drink were served to groups of workers as well as families, especially on weekend afternoons. The food was accompanied by tankards of beer. Most of the beers brewed in Chicago were made by Germans, but Edelweiss and later Meister Bräu were aimed particularly at the German population. Shots of schnapps or flavored brandies might occasionally accent the beer, the most notable of these being Bärenjäger, a strong honey apple brandy, and various forms of schnapps. Germans also drank other forms of German brandy, including Schaderer and Kirschwasser, as well as French brandies like Napoleon. For those who are interested, Jägermeister was not invented until 1934. Most of these brandies were imported from their home country. Today, Resi's Bierstube in the North Center neighborhood near Irving and Damen is an almost perfect example of the German beer garden. Unlike the "saloons" of other ethnic groups, German American beer gardens were mainly the domain of men, but during the afternoons, women and children were welcome to drop by and often did. The beer garden was a larger, partially outdoor part of the saloon. German music, culture and politics flourished at sites like Ogden's Grove, the Bismarck Garden and Edelweiss Gardens (the latter, originally called Midway Gardens, was designed by Frank Lloyd Wright), the Summer Bazaar Garden on the lakefront, the Heidelberg Gardens with its rock fountain and later the large German restaurant/bars, including Sauer's at 311 East 23rd Street, Zum Deutschen Eck near Lincoln and Southport and, most famously, the Berghoff.

The Czechs shared their language, pilsner beer and oftentimes radical thoughts and ideas in the bars of what is still called the Pilsen neighborhood, the "Checkefornia" area near 26th and California, and later bars and taverns in neighboring Cicero and Berwyn. They drank the local brews from the Czech-owned Atlas Brewery like Prager and later Czech imports. Other eastern European immigrants, most notably Serbians and Hungarians on Chicago's Southeast Side and Burnside neighborhoods, had a demand for Slivovitz, a plum brandy; Pálinka, a Hungarian fruit brandy; and Pelinkovac, a bitter liquor. They were probably made both "at home," in the form of simple pot stills or mixed with pure spirits and cooked on the stove or brought in from the old country by the suitcase. Later, local rectifiers would make cheaper knockoff versions of these liquors to cater to these populations.

The Polish who settled on "Polish Broadway," along South and later North Milwaukee Avenue, frequented former German or Irish taverns that—after years of hard boots walking on the floor, spilled beer, darts in the wall and sometimes fights where people were thrown out of windows—

were passed down or sold to owners catering to Polish immigrants. Among worn wooden floors, tables screwed together and smoke-stained walls, the Polish workers who drank there preferred beer, whiskey and a new entry into the local liquor scene: vodka or krupnik, a honey liquor not unlike mead. While many associate vodka as being Russian, there is evidence that the drink began in what is now Poland during the Middle Ages. According to the Polish Spirits Association, the world's first written mention of the drink and the word *vodka* was in 1405 from Akta Grodzkie, recorder of deeds in the court documents from the Palatinate of Sandomierz in Poland, and it went on to become a popular drink there. At the time, the word *wódka* referred to chemical compounds such as in medicines, cosmetics and cleansers, while the popular beverage currently known as vodka was called *gorzałka* (from the Old Polish verb *gorzeć*, meaning "to burn"), which is also the source of Ukrainian *horilka* (горілка). The word written in Cyrillic appeared first in 1533, regarding a medicinal drink brought from Poland to Russia by Russian merchants. Made largely from potatoes, the ingredients for vodka are cheap. Being a "new" alcohol that does not have to be aged, it is likely that many Chicagoans of Polish descent produced their own bootleg versions of vodka in the nineteenth and early twentieth centuries.

The Swedes, Norwegians and some Finns settled largely in the North Side neighborhood along Clark, Broadway and Ashland between Lawrence and Bryn Mawr still known as "Andersonville." As descendants of the Vikings, many of these immigrants were also hard drinkers. For this group, the main distilled liqueurs were mead, made from honey and originated in the days of Beowulf, and glogg. Still served during the holidays in Swedish bars today like Andersonville's "Simon's Tavern," glogg is made from red wine, spices and Aquavit. Aquavit is a form of bäskbrännvin, or Swedish liqueur made from wormwood. A Swedish immigrant named Carl Jepson would take the basic recipe of Aquavit and turn it into Malört. This liqueur was a staple of the Scandinavian population from the Great Depression into the 1980s. As described in later chapters, it would also take on a new life as the favorite drink of a new generation of "hipsters."

Not all immigrants drank beer and heavy spirits. Greek and Italian immigrants made up a large portion of Chicago's new arrivals in the early twentieth century. They generally settled in a neighborhood known as the Triangle, near Harrison, Halsted, Taylor and Racine. While Italians had their brand, "Prima" beer, Italian immigrants in Chicago generally tended to prefer wine, specifically red wine. These wines were usually made at home or by a friend or relative and kept in jugs.

A Chicago city tavern. *William Kralovec.*

The Greeks, once again generally, were similar. Just as in their native land, they did not frequent saloons, but rather tended to gather in coffeehouses, where they smoked, played cards, read Greek newspapers and drank espresso coffee late into the night. Wine and the occasional shot of ouzo would accent these gatherings, but alcohol was not the main attraction.

The Chicago Irish saloon was usually far different from Chicago German saloons or even the Irish pub. While Germans had food, tables, music, large windows and decorations, the typical Irish saloon consisted of the bar itself, a brass rail along the bar where people stood and drank and a few simple wooden tables. The interiors were often dark, with one widow in front, often painted over or obscured by signs. Whiskey, enjoyed in shots or small glasses, was the drink of choice. Beer was popular, but oftentimes its main function was as a "chaser" to the whiskey. While Chicago's Irish population dipped from 13.4 percent of the city in 1870 to less than 6 percent in 1900, 21 percent of saloons (1,256) were owned by the Irish.

The most famous or infamous of these saloon keepers were Irishmen "Bathhouse John" Coughlin and Michael "Hinky Dink" Kenna. The two became the aldermen and committeemen of Chicago's First Ward, as well as the "Lords of the Levee." The Levee was the nation's largest district of vice and prostitution. Kenna was the son of Irish immigrants who grew up near Polk and Halsted. John Coughlin, also the son of Irish immigrants, was born near Adams and Monroe. Unlike Kenna, Coughlin was six feet tall, with large arms and a barreled chest. As an older teen, he worked at a bathhouse on Clark Street and later at the Palmer House, hence his nickname. Here he handed out towels, shaving supplies and other items to Chicago's political movers and shakers of the time. In 1882, Coughlin opened his first bathhouse. That same year, Kenna opened his first saloon, the Workingman's Exchange. Kenna and Coughlin held power in their saloons well into the 1920s, serving as aldermen and committeemen of the ward, with Coughlin being elected in 1892 and Kenna in 1898. Coughlin served as alderman until his death in 1938. In a footnote to history, when Al Capone took over the area in the mid-1920s, he let Kenna and Coughlin continue to run their saloons. According to the book *Lords of the Levee*, Capone summoned a shaky Kenna to his office. In an odd moment of sentimentality and respect for what he basically saw as an old-school gangster, he told an old and weakening Kenna about how he had heard and read about their exploits, parties and past crimes. Capone told Kenna how much he enjoyed hearing these great stories, and he could continue to sell liquor in his territory.

As for Chicago's more landed gentry, who stayed in hotels like the Palmer House, dined in restaurants like Henrici's and lived first along Prairie Avenue and later in mansions along Lake Shore Drive and the "Gold Coast," there was a new way to not only consume spirits but also show your wealth: the mixed drink or cocktail. Cocktails first came into mainstream American and world culture in the 1860s. The publication of the first bartenders guide for cocktail recipes was in 1862: *How to Mix Drinks; or, The Bon Vivant's Companion*, by "Professor" Jerry Thomas, a bartender in New York. His book included recipes for punches, sours, toddies, flips and other drinks. Soon, other drink guides and new drinks followed. Among the earliest mixed drinks were the Old Fashioned, Sazerac and Manhattan. The term *highball* came into use during the 1890s to distinguish a drink consisting of one part spirits, one soda or mixer.

Another factor that led to the adoption of the cocktail was continued advances in refrigeration and the use of ice. After all, how many mixed drinks are there that do not contain ice? A man named Frederick Tudor is credited with the mass introduction of ice into American culture. Tudor perfected ways to cut blocks of ice out of frozen lakes and ponds in the North during the summer, store them in boxes insulated with hay and ship them, often to places like Florida and the American South. Tudor began this process in the 1820s and continued to improve on it during his lifetime. Just imagine how impressive it would have been to host a party in the 1880s on a hot summer day and, in a time before mechanical refrigeration, bring out a tray of whiskey or Sazerac cocktails topped with a cube or sliver of ice.

There was one area, however, where Chicago's wealthy industrialists came into closer contact with the shot-drinking, beer-swilling laborers: the First Ward, or the Levee District. Technically, the "old Levee" was located in what is now the south and west portions of the Loop and contained its share of whorehouses, bars and bathhouses. Although sex was the main

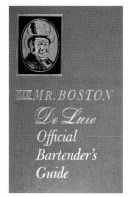
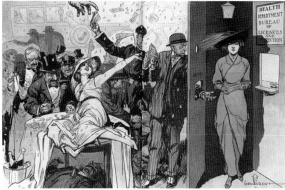

Left: *The Boston Bartender's Guide* helped to bring cocktails to America. *Photo by author.*

Right: The "Scarlet Women" from Chicago's Levee District. *Library of Congress Historical Photo Collection.*

attraction, alcohol came in second. Like with the brothels themselves, the range of alcohol varied from the high-class mansions that served cocktails to the smaller back rooms where shots of whiskey and rum were probably the order of the night. Sometime around the turn of the twentieth century, the Levee crept south. Maps of the area show that the district generally ran from Polk south to 22nd Street along Clark, Dearborn, Archer and State. The vice in this area was said to easily rival that of Storyville in New Orleans. Some of the more exclusive and well known of these venues included the Everleigh Club and the Victoria, owned by "Big Jim" Colosimo. Although authors like Richard Lindberg have written extensively about the Irish and other ethnic gangs of the late eighteenth century, Colosimo is recognized by most amateur historians as Chicago's first "gangster." An immigrant from Cosenza, Italy, Colosimo began his career as a precinct captain and later a "bagman" for Kenna and Coughlin. In 1902, he married Victoria Moresco, a madam. Together, they operated numerous houses of prostitution. "Establishments" with names like Bed Bug Row, the Bucket of Blood, Crib Houses, Japanese and the Why Not catered to the low-rent, no-frills whoremonger who drank cheaper whiskey.

As Colosimo's empire expanded, other gangs, including the Sicilian Black Hand, the forerunner to the mafia, began to pressure Colosimo. Although he was a large man himself, he hired a man who some say was his or Moresco's nephew, Johnny Torrio, from Brooklyn, New York, to help put together an organized gang. Also known as "Diamond Jim," Colosimo was known to enjoy opera, fancy clothes and "the good life," including running his own nightclub, Colosimo's. In the meantime, Torrio was busy at work organizing his gang. In 1919, he brought in a young man named Al Capone from New York to work as a bouncer in Colosimo's whorehouses. Many credit Torrio as being a mastermind of crime as well as business and one of the chief architects of the modern syndicate. In 1918, this business mastermind continued following politics and the news and saw a unique business opportunity. With the coming of Prohibition, Torrio knew that there would be a demand for booze. Even before the Eighteenth Amendment passed in 1919, this visionary businessman began setting up stills and bathtub gin operations and buying breweries throughout Chicagoland. Colosimo, who had since divorced Moresco and married a young opera starlet, apparently did not see the future in bootlegging spirits and would not commit the gang's resources. Instead, "Diamond Jim" continued his partying ways. Torrio would soon no longer accept Colosimo standing in the way of his plans for bootlegging. In May 1920, Colosimo was assassinated. A young Brooklynite named Frankie Yale was suspected of the murder, but many believe that Al Capone was also in on the job. With the Eighteenth Amendment ratified and Colosimo gone, the infamous era of Chicago bootlegging spirits began in earnest.

PROHIBITION

The Face of the City Changes Forever

No singular event has defined Chicago, its image and history more than Prohibition. Not just in the United States but around the world, Chicago is known as the "gangster city," the home of Al Capone. For many, mentioning the word *Chicago* elicits the formation of a make-believe machine gun, accompanied by a "*rat-a-tat-tat*" sound. Countless movies and TV shows, most notably *The Untouchables*, have fostered this reputation. For a brief period in the 1990s, Michael Jordan was able to eclipse this image, as Jordan's slam dunk pose and the red Chicago Bulls logo replaced the machine gun and fedora as our city's symbols. But after Jordan retired, Chicago slowly returned to being the gangster city. This is seen not only with the continued onslaught of movies and TV shows but with also the continued use of Capone's likeness throughout Chicagoland to promote everything from gangster tours, restaurants and nightclubs to barbershops and video games. The primary catalyst behind the rise of Chicago's most infamous citizen was alcohol—or, specifically, the lack of it.

The Eighteenth Amendment to the U.S. Constitution states, "After one year from the ratification of this article, the manufacture, sale, or transportation of intoxicating liquors within, the importation thereof into, or the exportation thereof from the United States and all territory subject to the jurisdiction thereof for beverage purposes is hereby prohibited. The Congress and the several states shall have concurrent power to enforce this article by appropriate legislation." Ratified on January 16, 1919, this bill took effect a year later, as on January 17, 1920, the Eighteenth Amendment and the accompanying Volstead Act became law.

Although the anti-alcohol forces had been fighting for this law for more than fifty years, two other amendments to the Constitution made Prohibition possible. The Sixteenth Amendment reads as follows: "The Congress shall have power to lay and collect taxes on incomes, from whatever source derived, without apportionment among the several states and without regard to any census or enumeration."

The story of Peoria and the Whiskey Trust tells the tale of the tremendous income derived by the U.S. Treasury from the taxation of whiskey and other alcoholic beverages. Some estimated that in its peak years as much as 40 percent of Uncle Sam's income was generated by these fees and that much of the Union debt from the Civil War was paid off as a result of "whiskey stamps." The Sixteenth Amendment partially freed the U.S. Treasury from its dependence on the alcohol taxes, in many ways helping pave the way for Prohibition. Although it came months after the Volstead Act was enacted, most believe that the Nineteenth Amendment, giving women the right to vote, was a forgone conclusion. Since women were the driving force behind much of the anti-alcohol movement, it is not unreasonable to surmise that

Bootleg whiskey ready to be shipped from a warehouse. *Library of Congress Historical Photo Collection.*

Prohibition was in some ways a political recognition of and concession to the women's suffrage movement.

In its enactment, the Eighteenth Amendment was a victory for the temperance and anti-saloon forces that had been fermenting for more than half a century. In Chicago, it was a victory for the memory of Levi Boone, who tried to close saloons on Sundays almost seventy years prior. It was a victory for Frances Willard and the WCTU. It was a victory for the politicians behind raising the liquor licenses, which began the "tied houses." It was a victory for the Anti-Saloon League, Billy Sunday and the Pacific Garden Mission. But it was a tremendous loss for the city of Chicago. The Eighteenth Amendment led to more than a decade of tremendous violence, corruption, murder, theft and terror caused by gangsters and gangs. Besides innocent bystanders being killed or injured in these gang wars, Prohibition also affected Chicago's citizens in many other ways. Hundreds if not thousands of Chicagoland residents were poisoned or suffered severe injury, including blindness or even death, through the consumption of wood alcohol and other toxic substitutes used in the making of unregulated alcoholic beverages. We have seen and heard the stories of Johnny Torrio, Al Capone, Bugs Moran, Hymie Weiss, Frank Nitti, Jake "Greasy Thumbs" Guzik and "Machine Gun" Jack McGuire and their violent struggle to control Chicago's making and distribution of illicit alcohol in countless books and film adaptations. This chapter will not rehash them. Instead, it will focus on their role in Chicago's history of alcohol and distilling and the effect that Prohibition had on it.

Even before Prohibition, the "Golden Age of Brewing" was ending. German and Irish immigration had slowed, and many of the first immigrants were moving out of the city's crowded ethnic centers to neighborhoods with tidy streets and homes, like Old Irving Park and Portage Park to the north and Beverly to the south. They were achieving a more middle-class lifestyle, and drinking, while not eschewed, diminished. The anti-German sentiment of World War I, as well as the trickle-down effect of the anti-alcohol forces, was taking its toll on the amount of beer consumed. While local beer consumption was taking a hit, the new decade ushered in a new market for distilled spirits. This came primarily through the new and more widespread consumption of mixed drinks or "cocktails."

If you view any posters, photographs or memes related to the Roaring Twenties, they generally show a woman in a flapper dress and high heels, legs in the air, holding a martini glass. In previous centuries, distilled alcohol was typically consumed straight, by men, usually in the form of a shot.

After all, how many cowboy movies have you seen where John Wayne bursts through the swinging doors, puts his hat on the bar and says, "I'd like a gin and tonic, lime on the side"?

By the time Prohibition rolled around, a good portion of America's northern, urban households had ice delivered on a regular basis and stored in an early refrigerator known as an "icebox."

The gangsters, bootleggers and basement distillers generally produced spirits that were far worse tasting than their professional counterparts, whose stills were now largely closed. Instead of whiskey, which often needs aging, they produced "bathtub gin," which is easier to make and can also be sold and served immediately. Even today, few drink shots of gin. So ice, fruit juices, sugar and other flavorings were added to mask the poor quality. These sweeteners were also important in that the 1920s saw women begin to drink spirits in the form of cocktails. Finally, alcohol in the form of spirits can have a faster and more immediate effect, as they can be consumed more quickly—an important factor in speakeasies, which could be raided at a moment's notice. So with wine and beer less readily available during Prohibition, spirits began to take their place.

But alcohol itself played a prominent role in these events and the history of Chicago in the Roaring Twenties. Since the city's first days as a trading post at Wolf Point, the manufacture, sale and trading of alcohol and alcohol-related products have been parts of the economic engine that drove the city. Just before Prohibition, a network of brewers and saloon owners lobbied both Springfield and Washington, citing job losses for brewers, truck and wagon drivers, bartenders, salesmen and coopers, as well as the impact this would have on Chicago's economy. It was estimated that Chicago would lose not only hundreds of jobs but also as much as $8 million in tax revenue. These complaints went unheeded. During the next decade or more, the money made by gangsters made that $8 million seem like "lunch money," and until Capone was convicted of tax evasion, the state, local and federal governments did not see a dime.

Chicago Begins Distilling Again—Sometimes with Deadly Results

Since the dynamiting of the Shufeldt Distillery in 1888, Chicago had more or less ceased production of whiskey or other distilled spirits. This changed with the coming of Prohibition, with unfortunate and sometimes deadly results. Like with the Chicago breweries, the whiskey production facilities in Peoria saw the coming of Prohibition and began to wind down. The first day of the new law saw most of them close. Two factors came into play. People still wanted whiskey. Unlike beer, whiskey and other spirits produced a much quicker, stronger and more lasting effect. This need was filled by a new breed of Chicago "distillers," who gave a new and deadly meaning to the phrase "staggering drunk."

Almost as soon as Prohibition was enacted, new stills sprang up like a cornfield in July in basements, garages and back alleys around the city. The term "bathtub gin" is more myth than fact, as the large copper or tin tubs that were used as wash basins before ceramic tubs were open vessels and could not effectively distill alcohol. Instead, copper pots, five-gallon olive oil tins, car radiators, copper tubing, old wood-burning stoves and empty water barrels were converted into tiny whiskey plants. The most numerous of these were set up by the Genna brothers along Taylor Street in the Little Italy section of Chicago. Already familiar with making wine, the Gennas provided sugar, yeast and sometimes a copper pot to Italian immigrants. Besides sugar and yeast, the homemade stills used potato and potato peels, corn and a bit of glycerin and juniper flavoring to make "gin." "Whiskey" was deemed such by adding a bit of brown syrup for coloring. They paid the "paesano" as much as $75 per week, or in today's money almost $1,000, for their services. Later on, Capone would expand these operations as well as open stills capable of making thousands of gallons of whiskey, rum or gin in warehouses across the city. Quality didn't matter, especially to the gangsters who made it and sold it. But in a way, the stranglehold of the Peoria whiskey distillers was finally broken, and whiskey, if you could call it that, was once again being distilled in Chicago.

Under the terms of the Volstead Act, individuals could also make up to two hundred gallons of wine at home for personal use. Many of Chicago's Italian, Polish, Serbian and other immigrants had already been making home wine for generations, so they just kept the apparatus going. For those not familiar with the process, grape growers found a way to make it easier. In grocery stores and fledgling supermarkets like A&P, they concentrated dried grapes into "wine bricks." They were sold with a very specific message that read, "Warning, if you were to put this brick in water and leave it for 21 days, it will turn into wine." Large markets and corner stores also sold yeast, malt, sugar syrup, barley and other materials needed to make beer at home.

Chicagoland distillers found other ways to get around the ban. In recent years, a liquor called Jeppson's Malört, or simply Malört, has become a cult

Whiskey seized from a Canadian vessel. *Library of Congress Historical Photo Collection.*

favorite among millennials and especially "hipsters," who have adopted it as their own. But just like fried chicken, ales and long beards, Malört was around a long time before the coming of the hipster. It is made from a Scandinavian recipe of wormwood, fruits and other herbs that has been around since the days of the Vikings. An immigrant named Carl Jeppson began distilling and selling it in the 1920s. Jeppson was a cigar shop owner who probably made the first batches in the back of the shop. He then began to peddle Malört out of a suitcase on the sidewalk. Because of its strong, medicinal taste, which some say resembled a pint of gasoline flavored with a stick of licorice, legend has it that whenever he was approached by law enforcement, one shot of the drink convinced the police that it was indeed an elixir capable of curing illness and stomach ailments if you did not die from it first. Nobody in their right mind would actually drink it unless they were deathly ill.

While many joked that such drinks would either "make you a fan for life or kill you," there was a true deadly side to the making of illegal alcohol during Prohibition. Since its inception, the red stamp on liquor bottles has identified them for tax purposes, but it also generally implies a modicum of safety. This, as well as the label on the bottle, indicates that it has been made by a reputable distiller with a name, address and place of business that can be identified. Prohibition changed all this. Just as illegal drugs are often "cut" with everything from sugar and baking soda to rat poison, a new, unscrupulous breed of profit seekers catered to a desperate market with sinister alternatives. This included the addition of wood alcohol, denatured alcohol, kerosene, benzene and other forms of alcohol used for manufacturing and not human consumption. The most common of these was wood alcohol. Wood alcohol is made from the distillation of wood, or technically the reaction between carbon monoxide and hydrogen. It is used in solvents such as denatured alcohol, and before glycol, it was a prime ingredient in antifreeze. Out of the host of alcohols, it is fast, cheap and easy to make. Even cheaper than old grain is old wood. Early bootleggers saw this immediately, and it wasn't long before Prohibition began that this deadly new twist began to take effect. On November 19, 1919, an unsuspecting whiskey drinker named William Boerst, age twenty-nine, entered a saloon at 4158 South Campbell Avenue, which was then part of a Polish/Lithuanian section of Chicago. He needed a shot, and after he drank it, he felt that period of relaxation. It felt good. But soon, something seemed wrong. Suddenly, his eyes started to water. When he tried to stand, he began to feel dizzy. His stomach felt like it was being cut into pieces, and his heart raced. What he did not know was that he had just drunk wood alcohol. While his liver was able to break down grain alcohol, wood alcohol turns into formic acid or formaldehyde. Soon, the dizziness turned into seeing blue and gray spots. Technically, the neurons in the parietal cortex in his brain, which processes vision, were being destroyed. All he knew was that when he opened his eyes, everything went black. Saloon owner John Weikus and bartender Tony Keriz were charged with manslaughter. This was also recommended by the coroner. In true Chicago fashion, however, the charges were "stricken off" on February 9, 1924.

Chicago's most infamous server of wood alcohol was Mary Wizeniak. A Polish immigrant, Wizeniak ran a speakeasy in La Grange Park, a small town just southwest of Chicago. Sources say it was run out of her home and well known to local customers. Whether or not she served tainted alcohol regularly has not been proven, but one night she served a customer, George L. Rhueutan, who fell into a nearby bog. Autopsies revealed that he had died from alcohol poisoning. Mary was thirty-four years old and a single mother of three. The fact that she was a female bootlegger garnered much attention in the press, which dubbed her "Moonshine Mary." Mary was given concurrent sentences of one year followed by life in prison, but after that, little was recorded about her. Like the vapors of alcohol themselves, Mary seemed to vanish into thin air. Wood alcohol being served to patrons wound up included as story elements in two episodes of *The Untouchables* TV show; episode no. 103, titled "The Snowball," features a young business major turned bootlegger, played by a then unknown Robert Redford, who sells poison hootch made from wood alcohol to students at Northwestern University. Like many of the *Untouchables* episodes, it has elements of fiction, but there were also plenty of facts to support the story, not only in Chicago but nationwide as well.

In January 2015, *Time* magazine reported that many of the most ardent supporters of Prohibition, including the Anti-Saloon League and Seymour M. Lowman, assistant secretary of the treasury in charge of Prohibition, actually supported a U.S. government–backed plan to *increase* the toxic elements in denatured alcohol. The January 10, 1927 issue of *Time* reported that "a new formula for denaturing industrial-grade alcohol was introduced, doubling how poisonous the product became." The new formula included "4 parts methanol (wood alcohol), 2.25 parts pyridine bases, 0.5 parts benzene to 100 parts ethyl alcohol," and as *Time* noted, "Three ordinary drinks of this may cause blindness." In the view of many, including anti-alcohol crusader Wayne B. Wheeler, those who were breaking the law did not deserve the protection of the government. "The Government is under no obligation to furnish the people with alcohol that is drinkable when the Constitution prohibits it," Wheeler said.

The results were tragic. In 1928, it was recorded that thirty-three people died from drinking poisonous alcohol in Manhattan. Surely many indigents and members of the poor and working class also ended up dead in Chicago. Few complaints were filed. After all, they died while breaking the law. Ironically, it was Capone's gangsters who played a major role in making sure that the "hootch" may have tasted like poison but was not actually poisonous. In the *Untouchables* episode, Redford's character is killed by Frank Nitti. This is fiction based on fact. While the mob's bootleggers were definitely not above killing, innocent people dying from alcohol poisoning was quite bad for business, and any "poison" sold on the streets was dealt with quickly and forcefully by the major syndicates. As the Roaring Twenties continued, the booze business in the Chicago mob was doing very well. Figures vary, but at the height of Capone's operation, it was noted that he had at least twenty breweries in operation making one hundred barrels of beer per day at $56 per barrel. Add in whiskey and gin, minus payoffs to police, judges, politicians and expenses, and Capone's organization was netting $75 million per year in alcohol sales. Capone was making lots of money, but there was one problem: he wasn't paying any taxes on it. On October 17, 1931, Capone, who had ordered or personally committed dozens of murders, was convicted of income tax evasion. While that did not stop Capone's gang and their bootlegging, the involvement of the federal government sent a message to his successors that, unlike the local officials, the "feds," who had a stronger hand in regulating hard alcohol, could not be as easily bribed. In December 1933, Prohibition was repealed, ending an era in Chicago history but laying the groundwork for new ventures in the alcohol business.

POSTWAR SPIRITS CREATE
NEW LIQUOR EMPIRES

A group of liquor distributors, rectifiers, salesmen and all-around hustlers assembled in a hotel meeting room downtown. A representative from a major liquor concern in Buffalo, New York, arrived to make a presentation on his new line. The room looked like a scene out of a Damon Runyon play, as men in off-the-rack suits, loud ties, sport coats and various hats and headgear chomped on cigars and generally shot the breeze. The representative from Buffalo touted his line, pointing to hand-typed sales charts, colorful labels and bottles of different shapes and sizes. Then came the highlight of the sales pitch: small amounts were passed around for the Chicago booze slingers to sample. One particular salesman, known as "Carload Friedman" because he traveled throughout the city selling booze to liquor stores and bars out of the back of his car, took a long sip of a vodka-type drink. He then took another. Recognizing a flavor that he knew would appeal to Chicago's typical working-class drinker, who was not particular in what he drank as long as it got him drunk, Friedman looked up and asked, "Does this shit come in half pints?"

Like many trends, it was not one but many events that created a new hard liquor landscape in Chicago. This landscape created another group of millionaires and multimillionaires with fortunes built on booze. This new class of liquor barons was partially responsible for the establishment of trusts and foundations that helped build hospital wings, community centers, theater companies such as the Goodman and Organic and the Chicago Blackhawks.

The first domino was, of course, the end of Prohibition. Hard booze no longer had to be made out of copper kettles in immigrants' living rooms or snuck in via midnight truck, often from Canada, accompanied by a cadre of men in long coats with .38s. Now it could come from anywhere.

But not from Peoria. Even before Prohibition, the Whiskey Trust was unwinding, but the passage of the Eighteenth Amendment meant that most of Peoria's major whiskey plants, with the exception of Hiram Walker's, dissolved like the water boiling off into steam on a still. While labels like Jim Beam and Maker's Mark boast histories of nearly two hundred years, the fact is that these labels were not always the giant corporations they are today. But post-Prohibition Chicago changed all that. While many factors were involved, trucks, new roads and a cadre of drivers helped place Tennessee and Kentucky whiskeys into the national forefront. Before the 1920s, liquor was largely made locally or shipped by river or rail from Peoria, a river and rail center. The mountains of Kentucky and Tennessee have scenic backdrops, old shacks and distilleries back in the hills. No riverboat or train tracks could make their way up and down to the backwoods country shacks. But throw an old tarp over the truck bed and head into town to meet a train or larger truck, and the next thing you know your whiskey is in Chicago, Las Vegas or anywhere else.

Another factor was the mob—or absence of it. During Prohibition, almost all the liquor supply in Chicago was controlled by criminal gangs, after 1926 almost exclusively by Al Capone. But as Prohibition ended, Capone, shocked and heading toward insanity, was placed in handcuffs and carted off to federal prison. Frank Nitti also received a short jail sentence for federal crimes. During Prohibition, Nitti ran Capone's entire bootlegging empire. But after Prohibition, Nitti noticed that because of the federal tax stamps and revenue, higher percentages of alcohol and greater price, federal agents or "revenuers" did not focus on the brewing and distribution of beer. Instead, they concentrated almost exclusively on hard liquor. After dealing with Eliot Ness and spending time in federal prison, Nitti wanted nothing to do with "the feds." So Nitti and Lou Greenberg concentrated the majority of their resources on beer and beer distribution like the Manhattan Brewery, leaving a space in the world of liquor.

"The 'revenuers' (federal alcohol agents) concentrated on hard liquor, as there was one present at most distilleries to check on amounts made, taxes levied and so on, on an almost daily basis. Nitti wanted nothing to do with this and concentrated on beer, which had far less federal oversight," noted

Jeffery Schecter, who worked in the liquor business during the latter part of that era. "After Prohibition, there was, in many ways, an open market for rectifiers and distributors to go into business and open up brands in Chicago in the 1940s, '50s and '60s. Schecter added:

> *A lot of this market was controlled by a young group of Jewish investors and businessmen like Harry Bloom and Lou Weiss, Ben Paul, and Abe, Ida and Fred Cooper, Lester Abelson, Oscar Getz, and Jerry Leavitt. Because they were German and Russian Jews, they could not easily get into the country clubs and arenas where many of the worlds of banking and other investment propositions were settled. But they learned that they could invest in warehouse receipts in places like Bardstown, Tennessee. While they did have to deal with the mob in many ways including distribution as the mob controlled the Teamsters, the bartenders and hotel workers unions, they could get into buying and distributing hard liquor and wine in stores, bars, and ethnic restaurants, which created an opportunity for them. Eventually, many of them turned this opportunity into fortunes that will last for generations.*

Schecter should know. His father, Abraham Schecter, had obtained degrees in both law and accounting from Northwestern University by the time he was twenty-two. Schecter hinted that despite his degrees, his father could not enter the established business worlds of banking and accounting, which were still controlled by old money, largely Protestant interests. So just as Chicagoans Leonard and Marshall Chess, two Jewish immigrants from Poland, made their own opportunity in a place where few would venture—Black or "negro" blues music—and changed American culture, many Jewish businessmen turned to the liquor business.

One of the first to venture into the arena of liquor sales, distribution and minor production were Abe and Ida Cooper. Just as gangsters like Johnny Torrio saw opportunity with the coming of Prohibition, the Coopers saw a new and open market when it ended. Abe and his wife, Ida Cooper, started Continental Distributing. Their business began out of the back of their cars, trying to work the ethnic markets. But soon it expanded, and eventually Continental became one of the largest liquor distribution companies in Chicago. Their son, Fred Cooper, took over and ran the company until 1996, when it was sold to Wirtz Beverage, Illinois. Cooper, however, continued to work at Continental under the Wirtzes. When Cooper died on April 23, 2011, among those who publicly mourned him was Rocky Wirtz, now chairman of Wirtz Corporation and chief executive officer of the Chicago Blackhawks, as well as Michael Binstein, president of Binny's Beverage Depot. Throughout their lives and after their deaths, the Coopers donated proceeds from the liquor business to many charities, most notably the Abe and Ida Cooper Center. Located at 6639 North Kedzie in Chicago, the center is a modern brick and glass structure. Catering to those of the Jewish faith, it provides counseling and psychological services for children who suffer from depression and abuse, as well as foster care for children who have been displaced from their homes or who have lost all support from parents and guardians. It also treats people with intellectual and developmental disabilities, providing home-based waivers for children and support and training for independent living, social activities, vocational and recreational classes and workshops, legal advocacy and personal care.

One way the Coopers and other non-connected investors gained entry into the liquor businesses was through buying or financing warehouse receipts. For many distillers, keeping whiskey for four to eight years can be expensive, as the costs of labor, materials and shipping are not recouped for the long amount of time that it sits during the aging process. Thus, distillers would sell the whiskey or other spirits as soon as they were made. In this way, the holder of the warehouse receipts "owned" the product but could not make good on the investment for the time it took to age the whiskey. The

The Cooper Foundation made much of its money from selling spirits and established this Jewish community center on Chicago's far North Side. *Photo by author.*

distillers, on the other hand, gained operating capital so they could continue to manufacture whiskey. "They would buy bourbon and vodka, oftentimes odd lots or merchandise they could not move, from anyone, and put a label on it," Schecter noted.

Instead, these liquor men were rectifiers. They took alcohol or neutral spirits and mixed them with other spirits, spices, sugars, prune juice, fruit and fruit flavorings, colors and dyes and made neutral spirits into brandies, vodkas, sherries, Amarettos and so on. The blends and tastes were not exactly like the originals, but these products were close enough, and combined with a substantially lowered price, fortunes were made off of products like peppermint schnapps, blackberry brandy, cinnamon-flavored schnapps or whiskey.

These rectifiers also produced "blended whiskeys." Unlike bourbon—which, like Champagne, has a legal definition of where, how and how long it is made—blended whiskeys are akin to "sparkling wines." The new breed of Chicago liquor men would go to places like Louisville, Cincinnati or other cities in the near south and purchase odd lots of whiskeys and blend them. "They would buy bourbon or maybe vodka from anyone and put a label on it," Schecter said.

Another family business that became a giant in the postwar liquor industry was started by Jerome "Jerry" Leavitt. Leavitt founded the Union Liquor Company on Chicago's South Side. His career began while working in his parents' grocery store when he was fourteen. His parents saw more money in alcohol and converted the store into a beer and liquor distributorship after Prohibition.

Leavitt became a rectifier and began producing liquors such as Henri-Ci's, but his big moneymaker was Dimitri Vodka. Often selling for half of what even the lower-quality brands sold for, Dimitri became the preferred drink for many whose fortunes and economic abilities had hit rock bottom. Known for the catchphrase, "It tastes so good you'd swear it was Russian," empty half pints and pints of Dimitri could be found in alleys, behind park benches and in the makeshift garbage cans of college students and at low-rent parties throughout Chicagoland from the 1950s until today. "Jerome had the Dimitri formula down," Schecter noted. "He would sell millions of cases of it a year, well into his death in the 1990s."

Another name or brand that blended the ethnic drinks like schnapps and flavored brandies was Many-Blanc. The company started in 1891, when Stanley G. Many began working at a South Loop liquor store. There he met Norris Blanc, a bookkeeper. Together, they opened a liquor and cigar

Peppermint schnapps was made by Chicago rectifiers, who blended simple peppermint with neutral spirits. *Author's collection.*

distributorship. According to the *Pro-Whiskey Men* blog, the partners distributed whiskey brands including Old Crow (Senator Mitch McConnell's favorite), Old Ethyl Bourbon and Mt. Vernon Rye. The company was located at several locations in Chicago's Loop, including 155 West Kinzie, 164 West Kinzie and 7–11 West Illinois. During Prohibition, they expanded their cigar business as they began manufacturing cigars. After Prohibition, the company was one of the first in Chicago to distribute rectified cordials, many under the Du Bouchett name. In 1945, the company was purchased by Schenley Inc. Today, Du Bouchett, part of Heaven Hill Brands, still churns out peppermint schnapps, peach liqueur and many more sweet, domestic cordials out of Bardstown, Kentucky.

Lester Abelson was another member of this group of young Jewish entrepreneurs who reestablished Chicago's liquor business after Prohibition. In 1933, Abelson and his brother-in-law, Oscar Getz, established Barton Brands. "Barton Brands owned such brands as Kentucky Gentleman Whiskey, and the House of Stuart scotch whiskey, and became successful not only in Chicago but across the nation," Schecter said.

In 1944, they bought Tom Moore Distillery in Bardstown, Kentucky, adding Tom Moore and Old Barton to their array of brands. They also established a brand called Very Old Barton. This whiskey was aged for as long as six years and became what may have been the first "premium bourbon." Today, there are hundreds of such brands, many aged eight years or more.

After World War II, they hired the young tax policy expert Abe Schecter and began producing products like Canadian Mist, Highland Mist and The House of Stewart Scotch.

Through these brands, Abelson and Getz slowly amassed a small fortune. Getz became a predecessor to many of the renowned whiskey critics of today, lecturing on whiskey and writing the book *Whiskey: An American Pictorial History* in 1978. He also opened the Museum of Whiskey History in Bardstown, Kentucky.

Abelson was able to achieve an even greater legacy, primarily through his wife, Hope Abelson. The Abelsons were married in 1933, about the same time that the Coopers, Leavitts and many others began establishing new lives and careers in the alcohol business. After raising two children, Hope Abelson got involved in theater and theatrical productions in the Chicago area, helping establish the Chevy Chase Theater in Wheeling, Illinois. In 1952, she teamed up with director Cheryl Crawford. Together, they produced and directed the Broadway version of *Camino Real*, written by Tennessee Williams and directed by Elia Kazan. She then produced *The Rainmaker*. One of the most successful plays of its era, it was made into a major motion picture starring Burt Lancaster. Needless to say, Abelson's career was off and running. She continued to produce and direct plays, becoming the grande dame of Chicago theater.

Combining the money earned from Lester's liquor empire and Hope's theatrical productions, the Abelsons graced Chicago's charitable and arts community with untold gifts and grants. Just a few of these include helping build the main stage and auditorium at the Court Theatre, which bear her name; the Goodman Theatre's Lester and Hope Abelson Fund for New Artistic Initiatives; Northwestern University's Hope Abelson Artist-in-Residence; and the Chicago Symphony Orchestra's Hope Abelson Artistic Initiative Fund. Other contributions to Chicago theater include donating a building that was turned into the Organic Theater at 3319 North Clark Street and countless smaller checks and donations to local theaters and productions for everything from costumes to paying the light bill. Other major charities the Abelsons supported include the American Cancer Society and the Chicago Community Trust.

The Abelsons also played a major part in the lives of the Schecter family. "My father got his start working for Lester Abelson who owned Barton Brands, which had brands like House of Stuart and Kentucky Gentleman which were sold across the nation," Schecter said. "He was an expert in taxation. He knew the tax policies, law, and accounting, but eventually got to know the other distributors nationwide."

In 1978, Schecter got into the business on his own through buying Medley Brands. Medley's roots trace back as far as 1634, when John Medley emigrated from England and settled in Maryland near the Potomac River in an area eventually called Medley's Neck. One of the ways Medley survived those hard winters and completely barren landscape was by making liquor from a homemade still. The newer generations of Medleys traveled to Washington County, Kentucky, and in 1812, they opened what was to be known as the Medley Distillery. Schecter bought Medley in 1978 and ten years later sold it to Glenmore Distillery. Today, it is part of the Sazerac Company, which is famous for its New Orleans cocktail that features Sazerac rye. Schecter continued to gain capital and in 1992 purchased Mar Salle Brands.

Mar Salle put out liquors such as Galliano Liqueur, Amaraita Amaretto and a local version of Pelinkovac. All three represent Chicago versions or local knockoffs of better-known national and international brands. Like many of the post-Prohibition sellers of spirits, Schecter's company did not distill anything.

One major change in the liquor industry after World War II that involved Chicago distributors was the mass proliferation of the large chain supermarket. In order to cut out middleman costs, these chains began to produce their own brands of items like coffee, canned goods and dairy products. This eventually spread into liquor. Grocery stores established their own brands, like Gold Coach Vodka, Skol Vodka and many others. Often contained in large half-gallon "easy pour" bottles that were later made of plastic, the grocery store brands fell into line with the Chicago rectifier tradition on booze making.

Schecter, however, was also involved with many "quality brands." "My father bought a bottling company in Kentucky from Cincinnati's renowned distiller Bob Gould which produced J.T.S. Brown whiskey.

Top: Sloe gin, a sweet liqueur that had little to do with actual gin, was used to make sloe gin fizzes. *Author's collection.*

Bottom: Mar-Salle Company may have been Chicago's largest mixer and distributor of spirits after Prohibition. *Author's collection.*

That became famous when Paul Newman's character, Fast Eddie Felson, developed a fondness for it in the movie *The Hustler*. In the movie he drank it straight from the bottle, and people remember Felson [Newman] ordering, 'J.T.S. Brown. No glass. No ice.' He was such a big star at the time, and him saying that did wonders for the brand."

An even bigger "star" in the bourbon world is Jim Beam. Today, its array of bourbon-related products makes it probably the most visible and popular of all Kentucky bourbon whiskeys in many areas. In 2018, the *Dayton Business Journal* ranked it as number four of the top twenty whiskey brands in America and the top-selling bourbon. But times have not always been so flush for Beam. During Prohibition, the distillery was closed entirely. Once again, it was Chicago investors Phillip Blum, his son Harry and later Harry Blum's son-in-law, Everett Kovler, who led a group of investors to purchase a major stake in Jim Beam during World War II. The book *American Still Life*, by F. Paul Pacult, notes that the Blums and their partners each put up the capital to buy controlling interest in the Jim Beam distillery. The agreement was similar to many made by Chicago's Jewish investors who ventured into the South to do business—Beam would run the distillery, while Blum would take care of sales, promotions and financing. "He let my dad run the show making the stuff. He took care of selling it," said Booker Noe's son, Fred.

Blum ran the company until 1959, when he turned over the reins to Kovler, a Chicago native who graduated from Lake View High School. Kovler's brainchild was to make Jim Beam the number one bourbon worldwide. Just as Scotch gained a certain cache with American drinkers during the 1960s, bourbon became a drink of choice for customers in Europe and especially Japan. The formula was that Booker Noe would make the bourbon and Kovler would sell it. Although the Beam bottle prominently features Noe and other Beam family members on the back, Blum and Kovler probably did not fit the image of bourbon, especially for many drinkers in the southern states.

In 1957, the profits from Beam and other liquor interests helped establish the Blum-Kovler Foundation. In 2016, it was reported that the foundation had $2.6 million in revenue and $46 million in assets. Among the grants listed for the foundation include funding several million dollars to the University of Chicago Koval Diabetes Center. Over the last decade, continual annual awards in the range of $600,000 to $700,000 were given to the John G. Shedd Aquarium, the Museum of Contemporary Art, the Lincoln Park Zoological Society, Millennium Park, the Jewish Metro Fund of Chicago, the North Shore University Health System and many others.

The largest and best-known of all post-Prohibition liquor distributing families is the Wirtz Corporation. Today, the Wirtz family generally ranks in the top one hundred in overall wealth in the United States. They are best known as owners of the Chicago Blackhawks, but their empire includes vast holdings in downtown Chicago real estate, a large stake in ownership of the United Center and alcohol distribution.

The Wirtz fortune exploded just before the Great Depression, when Arthur Wirtz began speculating with another future real estate giant,

Arthur Rubloff. While the Depression was a devastating blow to many, it was a boon to Wirtz. Having capital, Wirtz and James Norris, for whom the NHL's James Norris Trophy and Norris Division are named, began to invest in entertainment arenas. In 1937, they bought the Chicago Stadium and filled it with the proceeds from the Ice Capades, starring Sonja Henie, a three-time Olympic champion whose skating movies and shows made her one of the most popular stars of the 1940s. The two had a business relationship, and Henie helped Wirtz establish the first portion of his fortune with Norris. Wirtz went on to purchase other entertainment venues, including the St. Louis Arena and Madison Square Garden in New York City. In 1945, Wirtz purchased Judge and Dolph Liquor Distributorships from Walgreens Company, another Chicago-based corporation. Judge and Dolph was formed 1890, and the Wirtzes expanded the company. In 1955, it was earning $2.5 million and managed a ninety-five-thousand-square-foot facility on Clybourn Avenue in Chicago. They also purchased Edison Liquor. Soon Wirtz became the tenth-largest liquor distributorship in the nation and was responsible for delivering almost 50 percent of the liquor in Illinois. It is notable that Wirtz began to take control of the Chicago Blackhawks at about this time. While alcohol sales and distribution were not the sole financial reason why Wirtz was able to buy the team, it definitely played a major role. Arthur Wirtz died in 1983, and the family fortune was taken over by his son Bill Wirtz, who continued to increase the company's fortunes.

In 1999, the article "How the Wirtzes Sold Liquor Law" in the *Chicago Tribune* reported that Wirtz had grown into the eighth-largest beverage distributor in the United States, owning a collection of liquor distributorships in various states, including Judge and Dolph Inc.

Annual sales in 1999 were estimated to be about $750 million. A fortune to most, but just as many Chicagoans blame William Wirtz for mismanaging the Chicago Blackhawks and praise Rocky Wirtz for a new era that brought three Stanley Cups to Chicago. Rocky Wirtz also seems to have taken the Chicago-based Wirtz liquor holdings to new heights as well. In 2015, Rocky Wirtz combined the Wirtz-owned Breakthrough Beverage with Sunbelt Beverage. In 2017, Rocky and his son Danny Wirtz announced a deal merging Breakthrough with Texas-based Republic Distribution, creating a $12 billion liquor empire in more than twenty-seven states.

Today, we still see brands like Du Bouchett and Dimitri in liquor stores across the nation. Yet their roots go back to a group of investors and businessmen who catered to new markets across America, as well as familiar ethnic ones in Chicago. Starting from nearly nothing, their profits from the liquor industry were invested in real estate and other interests. Now the seeds that were planted selling sweet cordials and cheap vodka from the trunks of cars fund many of Chicago's major educational, cultural and healthcare facilities.

SKID ROW

The Darkest Side of Chicago Alcohol

Since the early days at Fort Dearborn and Wolf Point, alcohol sale and manufacture created fortunes for businessmen, helped drive Chicago's economy, made factory life more tolerable, gave immigrants a taste of home and fueled many a party. But for many, the party ended on Skid Row. In its heyday, if you walked down the 600 block of West Madison Street, you would have to wade through a sea of garbage and broken glass and have to step over men lying prone on the sidewalk or passed out in the gutter. On warm summer nights, the wind blew the stench of filth, vomit and urine up from the gutters and into your face. Signs, from neon to hand painted on wood, advertised cheap alcohol, cheap food, strip shows and flophouse hotels. When men were standing, they were usually holding paper bags with bottles, oftentimes with makeshift sheet bandages wrapped around their heads, the result of a fight with another "wino" or a fall on the sidewalk or down the stairs of a cheap hotel. The winter wind and snow may have disguised the stench and covered the garbage, but Chicago's brutal cold only made the situation worse. Men stood in doorways and alleyways or crowded flophouse hotels where they lived in six-by-four-foot "rooms" divided by sheets and chicken wire. In these rooms, germs hovered in the air like swarms of gnats as they coughed and vomited, passing germs from simple infections to full-blown tuberculosis. If you did not expire from disease or alcoholism, there was still a good chance that your body would end up stiff and frozen in a back alley, where police "paddy wagons" would make their rounds, tossing bodies in the back like cordwood.

Three Skid Row denizens enjoying a pint. *Photo by Tom Palazzolo.*

This is the area that *TIME* magazine called "The Land of the Living Dead," reporting on a series published by the *Chicago Daily News* documenting the experience of living on Skid Row. "The reporters took their readers on a guided tour of 46 flophouses, where 12,413 bums slept in lousy cubicles for 50¢ or 60¢ a night. They watched hard-faced jackrollers stripping the pockets and stealing the shoes from sodden bums, saw prostitutes plying their trade amid the lumber piles and back alleys.

Collier's magazine estimated that, circa 1949, the population of Skid Row was around seven thousand men in the summer and fifteen thousand in the winter. It went on to further describe Skid Row as "a jungle of crumbling tenements, twisted shacks and filthy alleys. It is an open jail for men who are guilty of no greater crime than being poor or not getting along with their wives, or just being lonesome." This was Chicago's Skid Row, the tragic and sometimes even fatal result of alcohol consumption. Skid Row generally ran from Lake Street south to Van Buren and from Clinton west to Damen with Madison Street as its epicenter.

"The whole West Side from Van Buren South to Lake Street was nothing but an area of boarded up businesses, flophouses, dive hotels, drunks, bars and burlesque houses," said Frank Pulaski, a Chicago writer and professed son of a safecracker for the "Chinatown Mob."

The term "Skid Row" takes its name from "skid road." The first use of the term can be traced to either Seattle or Vancouver, not far from the logging camps of the great Northwest. A skid road was the road that loggers used to drag logs through the woods. Later, it became known for the logging camps themselves. It was said that when loggers were fired, they were "sent down the skid road." Many times, loggers also sent logs skidding down chutes from a higher point down to a lower point or a river, where they were floated downstream. The analogy between sending a log "away" down a chute and a human being heading into a nameless oblivion is not a hard one to imagine.

Chicago's Skid Row most likely began at the turn of the twentieth century, when two major railroad lines ran along Madison Street and ended in the West Loop at Union Station. Railroad workers, often single men who traveled, needed a place to stay and perhaps have a drink near their home base. Hotels, bars, strip joints and burlesque houses catering to single workingmen sprang up along the avenue. Soon, the railroad men were joined by others, including migrant workers, ice cutters and part-time laborers who made their living along the rails. During the Great Depression, the group expanded to include hobos and gandy dancers. Gandy dancers earned their name from the dance-like movements they made as they kept the tracks aligned with rods produced by the Gandy Manufacturing Company. Unlike the bums, hobos and gandy dancers generally had their own code of conduct, usually eschewing severe drunkenness, violence and crime. The Great Depression and the resulting poverty, however, began to chip away at this precariously peaceful existence. The area became a no-man's-land that police mostly left alone, just as long as the crime did not make its way into the Loop. After World War II, thousands of servicemen returned home from the war. Some resumed normal lives with their families. Others—shell-shocked, lonely and suffering from what we now know as post-traumatic stress disorder—could find no counseling and turned to alcohol. It is estimated that many ended up on Skid Row.

"My father owned a combination pool hall, luncheonette at 661 West Madison, near Halsted," Diane Stratton said of the address, which would have been in the heart of Skid Row. "Sometimes he used to take us [his children] there and I remember the stench was so bad we used to roll up the windows. There was no AC back then but even in the sweltering summer we kept those windows up because besides the smell drunks would come up to the cars asking for a handout. I remember besides the drunks the area

A typical Skid Row street scene. *Photo by Tom Palazzolo.*

was always filled with soldiers and sailors who were there for the drinks and all the burlesque houses and skin shows." Stratton's father, Gus Georgulos, came to Chicago from Greece via New York. "My father owned three other businesses but the one on Madison was his cash cow.…It was kind of a fast food diner, with a pool hall in back, which was kind of scary, just men in a dark room, always smoke, bad smells, no light. I never went near there. The front part was the luncheonette. Most of the time men stood at the counter, and his biggest seller was hot dogs. Us girls always wanted to get a hot dog but my father would not allow us to sit out there. He would bring food to us back to the office, and I can see why. One time when we left and tried to get back into the car, some guy was taking a leak on the front tire."

Stratton's sister, Cleo Brown, also remembers her childhood trips, which were a combination of happiness for being able to spend time with her father, who put in long hours at the restaurant, which was open 24/7, and the horrors of Skid Row.

"I remember feeling uncomfortable, seeing people lining the gutters," Brown said. "Sometimes I think of my dad, who had to work there every day. It made money but it was dangerous. One day a drunk came in out of control. My father tried to calm him down, but he grabbed a bottle, cracked it in half and slit his face. He got kind of an Al Capone scar. That was the worst of it, but there was many a time he got hit on the head of with a piece of furniture trying to break up a fight."

Brown described how her father would sometimes try to help a customer. "Once in a while my dad would bring a guy to our house to do some work, painting a couple of rooms or something like that."

One man who almost gave his life to helping the denizens of Skid Row was Father Ignatius McDermott. Born in the Back of the Yards area after the turn of the twentieth century, "Father Mac" spent his childhood on the South Side of Chicago, especially the area around the stockyards. But he also lived through the deadly 1919 race riots, and on a lighter note, he even fetched a ball hit by Babe Ruth in the bowels of Comiskey Park. As a young man, he decided to enter the priesthood. But while attending seminary, he suffered a severe leg injury that kept him from graduating with his class. He was always a friend of the underdog, and his year of being partially disabled gave him an even deeper look into the souls of the disadvantaged.

Upon graduating from the seminary, he was recognized by Cardinal George Mundelein as a rising star. But Father Mac turned down more prestigious parishes to work near Skid Row. Night after night, Father Mac would walk Madison Street, hoping to save the souls of the many alcoholics. He was an early supporter of Alcoholics Anonymous, and Father Mac tried to get many of the men on Skid Row off the streets and into shelters. His work was recognized in the book *The Liquid Cross of Skid Row*, written by renowned sportswriter William Gleason.

But like the semi-fictional character "Tim" in the book, Father Mac was often not successful in his efforts. Just as there were many shelters promising salvation, there were also many day labor offices in the area. Here, men would line up every morning to make, at best, a few dollars washing dishes, cleaning out a garage or some other kind of short-term manual labor. But the men of Skid Row spent most of their time panhandling for money to get drinks. The men would usually gather in groups. In the documentary *Skid Row: Chicago's Madison Street in the 1940s*, the narrator describes how men got "a penny here, a dime there until they had enough for a bottle." Generally, a half pint would be shared by two men. If there were more, they would panhandle until they got a pint or even a fifth. Once they get enough money, the "hobo etiquette" stated that the largest contributor would get the first drink. If there were more than two men, the collection would continue until they got a larger bottle. Unless they spent the night in jail, which gave a man a special free drink, every man had to contribute toward the day's loot.

Men huddled on a winter's day in Skid Row. *Photo by Tom Palazzolo.*

The driving force in the lives of these men was alcohol. The "wealthier" men on the row—pensioners, semi-skilled tradesmen and those who had yet to be robbed—drank hard liquor, such as whiskey, gin, rum and, later, vodka. Favorite whiskeys included Phillips, Fleischmann's, Rich & Rare Canadian and Kentucky Deluxe. They also drank Chicago-area brands of gin and vodka like Dimitri's, whose tagline used to be "If it wasn't for the price, you'd swear it was Russian."

Cheaper brands of beer sold in taverns along Skid Row included Blatz; Ballantine Ale; Red, White & Blue; Stag; and Drewrys. Among Chicago's local breweries were brands like Fox Deluxe, Bismarck Beer, Bullfrog Beer and Ambrosia Lager Beer. But beer was not the drink of choice along the Row. Low-end and fortified wine largely fueled Skid Row. The list includes now-defunct brands like Ripple and Sly Fox. But many are still around. Richards Wild Irish Rose, introduced in 1954, is available in 13.9 percent and 18 percent alcohol by volume and sells almost 2 million cases annually. According to Bumwine.com, the "kings of Skid Row," Thunderbird and Night Train, are also still widely available in liquor stores today.

Many who were around during the 1950s and early '60s remember the radio jingle for Thunderbird that went, "What's the word? / Thunderbird / How's it sold? / Good and cold / What's the jive? / Bird's alive / What's the price? / Thirty twice."

It's likely no coincidence that the song doesn't comment on the wine's taste. Most remember it as terrible tasting and that sometimes the pale-yellow wine could turn your lips and mouth black. In a primitive precursor to the internet or phone surveys that are now done after almost every time you use a service or product, the owner of Thunderbird, Ernest Gallo, allegedly drove through Los Angeles's Skid Row, and upon seeing a homeless person drinking, he called out, "What's the word?" The person enthusiastically responded, "Thunderbird!" Apparently, as long as he heard the reply, he would continue to run the ads. When he did not, he began a new campaign.

"I remember the favorite on Skid Row was a wine called Muscatel," said Frank Pulaski. "There was also Boone's Farm and a brand called Mighty Fine Wine. These guys usually didn't care what they drank, as long as it was in a bottle."

But when times got really bad on Skid Row, the winos turned to even more sinister potions to feed their addictions. They drank Vitalis and other hair gel tonics and later Nyquil for their alcohol content. Many of the winos found part-time work washing dishes and got their hands on cans of Sterno, used to warm steam tables. Most of the time people used the cans to heat street corners, doorways and small enclaves during the cold Chicago winters. But when wine wasn't available, Skid Row residents reduced the solid "canned heat" into a liquid by straining it through a stocking. The result was a highly toxic cocktail known as a Pink Lady.

Richards Wild Irish Rose, along with Thunderbird and Boone's Farm, were fortified wines popular along Skid Row. *Photo by author.*

Before ethylene glycol, cars used wood alcohol or methanol in their radiators as antifreeze. On many a night, police caught folks draining the wood alcohol to drink. Known as Jake, wood alcohol did not provide the sense of relaxation usually associated with drinking alcohol. Instead, it provided a dull, numb high, often followed by unconsciousness. As time wore on, the wood alcohol began to attack the drinker's central nervous system. Many of the citizens of Skid Row who worked day labor came to recognize the effects of Jake. Workers' legs began to shake uncontrollably—called

"Jake Leg." It was the first in a series of tragic symptoms that often ended with men dying like rats on D-Con, their whole nervous system having broken down.

Once drunk or high, the men, often stumbling or on the verge of passing out, would head to a series of cheap hotels called flophouses and often sporting names suggesting paradise and fantasy. Even today, old-timers still reminisce about haunts like the Workingman's Palace, the Gem, the Starr Hotel, the New Norway and the Portland. Gleason's *The Liquid Cross of Gold* describes the Workingman's Palace as "[o]ne of the most prestigious addresses on the street. Its permanent (more or less) residents are members of the affluent society....For those who still write an occasional card to the folks back home. 'The Workingman's Palace' sounds pretty ritzy to relatives or friends in Alabama, Arkansas, or Montana who have never seen West Madison Street. The Workingman's Palace has a facility that sets it apart from less opulent flophouses. Guests who dwell on the upper floors don't have to worry about how to navigate the stairways when they are carrying a cargo of muskie. They can travel in style in an elevator."

But the Workingman's Palace was indeed a "palace" compared to many of the other Skid Row flophouses. The rooms, usually six by four feet and topped by chicken wire, were dubbed "bird cages." The nicer rooms had windows, doors and electric lights. Besides winos, the only regular visitors to these hotels were the Chicago police, who picked up ne'er-do-wells and drunkards in a paddy wagon, and hearse and ambulance drivers, who made daily rounds, moving the dead and dying to paupers' graves.

But that wasn't the only way men died in these hotels. The Barton Hotel fire was one of the most tragic in Chicago history. The fire was reported to have been started by a resident named Tony Armatayz, a seventy-year-old pensioner who began to rub alcohol on his body while smoking a cigarette. The alcohol caught fire, and he ran through the hallways. Maintenance man Tony Dykes said he ran through the building like a "human torch." An Associated Press article from February 13, 1955, reported on one of the many tragedies that occurred on Skid Row: "Fire, believed to have been started by a panic stricken, 'human torch,' sped through a crowded skid row hotel in sub-zero cold early Sunday morning killing at least 25 men. Fifteen, including two firemen, were injured. Most of the victims were derelicts or transients. Starting at 2 AM the blaze caught most of the hotels 245 roomers asleep in their tiny cubicle rooms separated by corrugated iron walls and covered with chicken wire....Coroner said he was horrified by the cooped up conditions of the hotel."

The New Jackson Hotel, one of the last bastions of Skid Row. *Photo by author.*

Reportedly, the Barton Hotel at 644–48 West Madison was owned by a woman and leased to the Gandy Hotel Company, which in turn subleased the property to two brothers, Benjamin Glassman and Max Glassman. According to Chicago Building Department files, the place was divided into sleeping stalls for 336 persons—48 were on the second floor, 85 on the third, 117 on the fourth and 86 on the fifth. The ground floor was occupied by the Standard Store Fixture Company. It is estimated that 245 men were asleep in the five-story building at the time of the fire. Their "rooms" were cubicles about four feet wide, six feet long and seven feet high. The bunks were separated from one another by corrugated iron sheets topped with meshed chicken wire. An aisle ran between each two rows of cubicles. The chicken wire was to provide ventilation and to keep the flophouse denizens from crawling into one another's cubicles.

Despite the alcoholism and deplorable conditions, another indisputable fact about the area was that not all men on Skid Row were losers. Many of the men, even the ones police ran into, often had families and formerly worked white-collar jobs. "The people down there weren't all bums," Pulaski said. "Some of the people were doctors, some lawyers. It was the classic American story of the time, how a man falls from grace."

Looking through the lens of time, many Skid Row occupants were World War II veterans who would now be described as suffering from post-traumatic stress disorder, or PTSD. In those days, it was called "shell shock." Help was available from organizations such as the Salvation Army or the Pacific Garden Mission, but it consisted mostly of giving men soup or doughnuts and a bed in a room crowded with other winos and thieves. In return, they were bombarded with religious sermons stressing punishment and resolution of sin. The Pacific Garden Mission still broadcasts the live radio drama *Unshackled*, which preaches, "Christ can break the fetters of sin and set the sinner free."

In 1963, Father Mac founded the Central States Institute of Addiction (CSIA), turning his efforts on the streets into an institution that provided resources for individuals and groups who helped people with addictions. Father Mac established the CSIA just as America was beginning to better understand addiction and undergo a sea change in attitudes. During the 1960s and '70s, Americans' ideas toward "bums" began to change. Alcoholism was soon seen as a family disease, and alcoholic men were no longer kicked out of their houses and sent to Skid Row; instead, they were referred to treatment. The advent of the automobile also changed Americans' attitudes. Before the car-centric, suburban age of the 1960s, men confined to places like Skid Row were largely isolated from the rest of the city and society as a whole. The widespread use of the automobile, however, led to drunk driving and the resulting deaths of drunk drivers and their victims. Politicians, businessmen and landowners faced ever-mounting pressures to tear down Skid Row.

Greed led to the ultimate demise of Skid Row. In the article "Public Dollars and Private Interests: How Skid Row Fought Back Against Chicago's Private Developers," published in 2004 in the housing and development magazine *Shelterforce*, authors Tiffany A. Meier and D. Bradford Hunt looked into the motivations behind urban-renewal plans for the six-block parcel at the heart of Skid Row. "For 10 years, the site languished as various schemes fell through. Businesses were closed, SRO residents were evicted and buildings were demolished, leaving a blighted landscape for most of the 1970s. Finally, in 1979, the city embraced the idea of Presidential Towers....The developers designed Presidential Towers as a $233 million self-contained community, hermetically sealed from what remained of skid row."

Heavyweight politicians involved in the scheme included developers Daniel J. Shannon, James P. "Jack" McHugh and Daniel E. Levin, as well as Mayor Jane Byrne, Tenth Ward alderman Ed Vrdolyak and Marina City developer Charles Swibel. According to the article, the city gave developers $180 million in federally tax-exempt city revenue bonds, and the Federal

The neon sign advertised a warm place to escape Chicago's hard winters. *Photo by author.*

Housing Authority granted developers a $159 million federally insured mortgage. Other breaks, including an exemption from the federal law that requires developers to set aside 20 percent of the units for the economically disadvantaged, were drafted by Chicago congressman Dan Rostenkowski, who was at that time chairman of the powerful House Ways and Means Committee. At the end, Meier and Hunt ask, "Was it good public policy to spend substantial federal and local resources to fund a privately owned redevelopment project for young professionals while avoiding any responsibility for low-income housing or for displaced skid row residents?"

Meier and Hunt's answer is no, but for most, the answer was yes. During the '80s and '90s, the former shacks, hotels, bars and businesses along Madison Street fell like dominos. The new United Center ushered in a series of bars, restaurants and, later, housing along what was once Skid Row. But the coup de grâce was Oprah Winfrey's Harpo Studios at 1058 West Washington, which was established in 1988. The land was cheap thanks to the location, but the coming of Oprah meant that stars like Tom Cruise and Halle Berry would be walking on the same sidewalk where winos once stumbled through broken glass and garbage.

Today, there are only a few signs that Skid Row once occupied most of the West Loop. Father Mac's Haymarket Center stands at 932 West

Washington, a block east of Harpo Studios. The Salvation Army's Rehabilitation Center is also close by, at 506 North Des Plaines, as is the new home for the Pacific Garden Mission at 1458 South Canal Street.

The "heyday" of Skid Row—the 1940s, 1950s and 1960s—coincided with the operation of Chicago breweries like Manhattan, Ambrosia and many others. But as these breweries closed in the 1960s and 1970s, Skid Row began to shrink in both size and severity. Businesses like Rothchild's Liquors may have survived well into the twentieth century, and Skid Row did manage to hang on in some form or other into the 1980s—a good decade longer than Chicago's major breweries and Chicago's brewing industry as a whole—but for all intents and purposes, Skid Row was done.

MALÖRT–CH DISTILLERY PLANT

Chicago's Legendary Hometown Liquor

On June 21, 2019, Mick Jagger took a break after a set that proved that, at seventy-six, he and the Rolling Stones still had the swaggering charisma that has affected popular culture for sixty years. Wearing a black-and-white checkered jacket, he stood onstage at Soldier Field and exclaimed to an audience of seventy thousand people, including myself, "We have played Chicago thirty-eight or thirty-nine times, and I still haven't had an Italian beef or a shot of Malört."

The fact that the crown prince of rock-and-roll singled out having a shot of Malört as a "must do" while visiting Chicago is a testament to the product. If there is one distilled liquor that has captured the history, identity and drinking culture of Chicago, it is Malört.

Like Chicago itself, Malört is not calm or pleasant. Sipping a shot, the first thing you feel is a sense of fire that hits your gums and the back of your throat. But unlike bourbon whiskey, which is accompanied by a thick, smokey sensation that you can savor in your mouth, Malört gives your taste buds a bitter, medicinal blast that comes across like Listerine or cough syrup. Then the final swallow goes down your esophagus and stomach like a piece of hot charcoal. The parallels to Chicago's identity are so intertwined that it is no wonder the city has adopted it. While California has its mellow wines, made with grapes grown on rolling, sun-swept hills and Tennessee and Kentucky have their whiskeys, strong and tough but made from nearby clear stream water and locally grown corn, Chicago has Malört.

Established in 1934, it is the oldest locally produced liquor. As mentioned earlier, many ethnic liquors were blended by rectifiers, who took neutral spirits shipped from places like Indiana and Kentucky, added flavors, a label, bottled it and called it "vodka." But aside from a few years when it was made in Florida, Malört has always been a Chicago product, identified with and by Chicagoans as a part of the city's fabric. For decades, it was a deeply kept secret. Bars kept it on the back shelf, where it was enjoyed by Scandinavians who settled in Wicker Park, Humboldt Park, Logan Square and later the far North Side area still known as Andersonville. In these ethnic bars, tradesmen of Polish, Slavic and other European descent watched their Scandinavian counterparts enjoying the beverage and began to favor Malört. Among men, it was considered the manliest of drinks. Young workers gained acceptance by being able to down a shot of Malört without coughing, wincing or spitting it out. "Here kid. Have a shot of Malört. It will put hair on your chest."

Then, as the new millennium dawned, a curious cultural transformation occurred. Perhaps because they also resided in the Wicker Park and Andersonville neighborhoods, college students and recent graduates who would eventually be known as "hipsters" began to adopt Malört as their own standard for manhood and later womanhood. College parties in the '80s and '90s were known for their love of Jägermeister. In many ways, it was strong like cough syrup, but it was also sweet. Consumed ice cold or in Jell-O shots, it evolved from a strong shot to a sweet sundae. Malört was stronger. Thus, it became the Chicago version of this party drink—stronger and more unique. On November 7, 2020, when young people flocked to Trump Tower to celebrate the election of the Biden-Harris ticket, the news media featured photos of the mostly twentysomethings popping not bottles of Champagne but Malört.

Malört's origins are derived from *beskbrannvinn*, a Swedish liquor with supposed medicinal properties. While beer, wine and many other forms of liquor have been around since the earliest days of civilization, *beskbrannvinn*, which is sometimes shortened to "Bask," is a relative newcomer. Distilled from wormwood, it is listed in many accredited medical journals as having medicinal properties. It was said to help with nausea and menstrual cramps, and a shot of Malört in the morning is also thought to be a good way to cure a hangover.

"As a form of liquor, Bask came late, in about the 1700s, but didn't take off until after Napoleon in the 1830s," said Peter Strom, a Scandinavian scholar and former part-time employee at Malört. "When it did come, it took off like Meth. Everyone had a still. It practically destroyed their society."

Malört featuring a replica of Chicago's flag—maybe Chicago's oldest spirit. *Dan Janes, CH Distillery.*

This may have been the way that young Carl Jeppson was exposed to Bask. He hailed from Ysted, located in the southernmost tip of Sweden, best known for its architecture and monasteries preserved from medieval times. A cigarmaker by trade, Jeppson arrived in the United States in the late 1880s. He settled on North Clark Street in what was a burgeoning Swedish community. Like with the "bathtub gin" of the era, Jeppson made Malört in small batches, probably in a back room, basement or garage. But unlike the primitive gins and "whiskeys," which were basically watered-down grain alcohol with perhaps a little flavoring, Jeppson must be given a lot of credit for formulating a drink composed of aged wormwood and other ingredients to form an actual liquor in such sparse conditions. "Carl sold door to door, bar to bar; it was basically a Swedish racket, sometimes sold as medical alcohol or sacramental wine," Strom said. "Probably his largest customer was Walgreens, which at that time owned over twenty pharmacies that sold Malört as a medical liquor."

Local legends have it that Chicago police officers stopped Jeppson while peddling Malört, took one sip and said something to the effect of "anything that tastes this bad has to be medicine." Strom and others are skeptical that this is a true story, but the embellishment does conveniently describe the taste of Malört to many.

As he was an immigrant working semi-underground selling cigars and Malört, details on Jeppson's life are sketchy. Strom suggested that Jeppson's last address was in West Rogers Park. "He died sometimes during the 1940s, and there was visitation and a funeral service at a funeral home near Foster and Clark," Strom said about the "Andersonville" area, which still maintains its predominantly Scandinavian identity. "There is no grave site or tomb so apparently he was cremated. He did have a son, and apparently his grandson found some of this information about him in the attic, but his life was in many ways a mystery."

The Malört website states that a company named Bielzoff Products bought the recipe for Malört at the end of Prohibition. The company's vice-president, a man named George Brode, bought out the company in the early 1940s. Brode was a 1933 graduate from Northwestern Law

School. Throughout his life, he manufactured and sold liquor as a hobby. His children told the *Chicago Tribune* that in 1933 he left the cap off of a bottle of Grenadine, and the red syrup fermented. Shortly thereafter, he legally produced "Red Horse Liquor" at a small plant on Rush Street and the Chicago River in the 1930s. The operation was tiny, a hobby, but Brode discovered that there was money to be made and began experimenting with other small-batch "basement" liquor concoctions. "Brode was fascinated with Malört, and he tried different recipes and versions of it," Strom noted. "It was still made in Chicago at a distillery at 11th and State."

A bottle of Malört. *Dan Janes, CH Distillery.*

The exact location and name of exactly where Malört was actually made during all these years also remains somewhat of a mystery. Patricia Gabelick, Brode's legal secretary and eventual owner of Malört, stated in an interview with the author in 1997 that during the 1940s, Malört was made at the Red Horse Distillery, first at Rush and Wells but probably moved to the one Strom said was located at 11th and State. Gabelick noted that during the 1950s, the product was made at what she simply called Brode Distilleries on 31st Street. The Malört website notes that in 1953, Brode entered into an agreement to produce Malört at the Mar-Salle Distillery, which was primarily involved in labeling, bottling, packaging and the mixing or blending of spirits. It is quite possible that Malört was at times made at both, as Malört continued to be somewhat of a "mom and pop" small-batch operation, surviving batch to batch, season to season. After hiring Gabelick in 1966, Brode began ceding more and more of the business of Malört to his secretary, concentrating more on his law practice as a probate attorney from an office located on the 200 block of North Wells Street.

In 1986, Malört, perhaps the only spirit to be entirely produced in Chicago since Prohibition, moved its operations first to Kentucky and then to Florida, thus ending its time as the only liquor distilled in Chicago since Prohibition. "Our offices, distribution, promotions, manufacturing and packaging are still done in Chicago," Gabelick said in an interview with the author in 1998. "So we are definitely still a Chicago product."

Like the alcohol itself, Malört's popularity continued to slowly ferment during these years. Hard-living tradesmen, seeing the popularity in some North Side bars, began adopting the drink as their own. This probably started as early as the 1940s and '50s. "The Poles came here and recognized it as something similar to a drink they had called Pilibnoika, and some of the Polish bars in Wicker Park and later along North Milwaukee Avenue began carrying it," Strom said. "Some of the Puerto Ricans who moved to Wicker Park also began to drink it, as it resembled Pitorro, a very, very strong home-type brew that many families make as a tradition during the Christmas holidays."

For the same "macho" reasons, the drink became popular with bikers, who would bring bottles of Malört from Chicago to bike conventions in cities like Sturges. In the 1990s, shots of Jägermeister became popular on college campuses around the Midwest. Soon, the students and young millennials hipsters began to find Malört. One of the main reasons was because, unlike the sweet Jägermeister, which went down easy, watching somebody drink Malört was a lot more fun. With the advent of social media, young people started posting pictures and later videos of unsuspecting drinkers convulsing in what is now known widely as "a Malört face."

Brode died in 1999. While his son George Brode II continued the law practice, Brode deeded the entire Malört enterprise to Gabelick, who continued to run the business out of her Chicago apartment near Belmont and Sheridan. During this time, it is estimated that Malört's sales went from 1,600 cases in 1999 to twice that in 2012—and more than 10,000 in 2017.

One of those social media contributors was a young man named Tremaine Atkinson, aka Sam Melching, whom the Malört website lists as printing T-shirts and other Malört products. Eventually, Gabelick found out about this enterprise. She apparently threatened to sue, but Atkinson charmed his way out of the situation, and the two became friendly. Atkinson was already familiar with the liquor business, as he owned CH Distillery, an up-and-coming business that made small batches of vodka and other spirits. Atkinson began to work part time, helping the aging Gabelick with marketing, especially in the realms of the new millennials and social media, of which Gabelick had little knowledge. Due to the rising popularity and tripling of sales, the company was actually having trouble finding a larger source of wormwood, a problem that Atkinson helped solve. After several attempts in the next five years, Gabelick finally relented and sold the recipe, rights and enterprise of Malört to Atkinson and CH Distillery in 2018.

"Tremaine Atkinson, who owned CH Distillery, was a fan of Malört and saw Gabelick at a spirits event where he inquired about buying the label," said Dan Janes, a part-time publicist at the label, in a 2019 interview. "Gabelick declined, but Tremaine kept asking, until one day Gabelick

The CH Distillery, located on Chicago's near South Side. *Photo by author.*

approached him and said she was retiring and decided Atkinson would be the right person to continue the Malört tradition."

In 2018, the CH production plant, located at 1629 South Clinton Street, began receiving truckloads of wormwood, which resembles tumbleweed, according to Janes. By the spring of 2019, Malört was not only owned, shipped and marketed by Chicagoans but also once again produced in the Windy City. Thus, we will excuse the short break in the 1990s and still extol Malört as being the oldest continually produced local liquor in Chicago.

THE THORNTON DISTILLING COMPANY

John Kinzie, Al Capone, Brewing and Distilling

The building stands on the banks of the Thorn Creek in Thornton, Illinois. For hundreds of years, American Indians camped along the creek, enjoying the fresh, springlike waters. When the area was settled, the spring water and artesian well was used to brew beer for more than one hundred years, sometimes under the "ownership" of Al Capone. But on a hot August night in 2021, guests sat in an exposed brick courtyard under Italian lights, sipping cocktails like the 20th Century Limited and One Way Ride, made from spirits distilled from the water that runs from the creek in underground caverns into a well practically underneath their tables. Inside the main bar, known as The Well at the Distillery, the building still contains the roughhewn lumber floors and beams; high, barnlike ceilings; and many other features that owner Andrew Howell has maintained from the original structure. Built 175 years ago, this former brewery turned distillery has seen history, including ownership by John H. Kinzie, German and Irish immigrants, artesian wells, horse-drawn wagons and Prohibition days, when it was run by Joseph Soltis, Public Enemy No. 9 and a lieutenant for Al Capone. While it is impossible to sum up the history of Chicago and alcohol, much of this lore is contained at one site: the Thornton Distilling Company.

Located twenty-five miles southeast of Chicago in the small village of Thornton, the distillery sits on the site of the oldest standing brewery in Chicagoland. While most of the brewery's history may fit neatly within the profile of Chicago breweries, there is one major difference: limestone caves.

The Thornton Distillery was a haven for early settlers and Al Capone and his henchmen, and it is now a craft distillery. *Photo by author.*

The business sits less than half a mile from the outskirts of the Thornton quarry. One and a half miles long, half a mile wide and more than 450 feet deep, it contains Silurian reefs, which were formed when the area was covered with salt water 400 million years ago. It is adjacent to the Tri-State Tollway, and thousands of drivers a day ride by its cream-colored walls, which seem to stretch down forever. The lower level of the distillery also comprises these limestone caves. Andrew Howell, cofounder and chief executive officer of the distillery, sees them as a major part of the operation. Their entrance resembles that of a medieval prison cell, as a thick wooden door and damp stone stairs lead down into the caverns. A plaster relief of what looks to be the Greek face of comedy/tragedy has been festooned over it for further decoration.

"It used to be the largest quarry in the world," Howell said, "but recently they opened up a bigger one in China." Walking farther, a large, capped pipe sticks out of the ground. Surrounded by a cement bed, this is the artesian well that was the main catalyst for what became almost 150 years of brewing.

"There was a natural, underground spring here," Howell noted. "It was discovered and used by the Native Americans, who marked it with a pointer tree which is near the property. They had encampments along the Thorn Creek, which is just across the road, and the spring was one of their major gathering spots."

Evidence of Native American occupation along the creek dates back to AD 1400. As the township became settled, evidence of Indian fortifications,

The water for much of the spirits is drawn from an artesian well that has been used since the days when Native Americans populated the region. *Photo by author.*

flint arrowheads and other tools were found. In 1835, John H. Kinzie platted the town. One year later, Kinzie, John Blackstone and Gurdon Hubbard opened a sawmill, and Hubbard began to mine the limestone that would eventually become the Thornton Quarry.

"John Bielfeldt, a German immigrant, built this structure and opened a brewery here in 1857. About ten years later this became a railroad stop, and the brewery became a roadhouse, marked by blue lanterns or red lanterns to signal the railroad workers," Howell said. "Between that, the building of the I&M Canal and the establishment of the quarry, the Bielfeldt brewery was booming. The roadhouse soon turned into four buildings, including a cooperage, icehouse, brewhouse and bar. There was also a stables area where the draft horses that delivered the beer were quartered, and the horses and carriages of the men who visited would be tied up along rails in front or if they stayed for a long period of time, were housed in the stables."

Located in faraway Thornton, Bielfeldt was able to escape many of the anti-liquor laws and statutes passed in Chicago that led to the necessity of tied houses and other hurdles. The brewery thrived through the turn of the century and World War I, as it is said that the limestone from the Thornton Quarry helped build many of the structures used in the Burnham Plan. Even today, there is limestone from the quarry in buildings throughout Chicago. But while Thornton's distance provided a haven from the protests and politics of groups like the WCTU, it could not escape Prohibition. After almost seventy-five years, the Bielfeldt Brewery was closed in 1920.

But while Prohibition proved to be a bane for honest businessmen like Bielfeldt, it was a boon for a new generation of criminals and gangsters who called themselves "brewers." In the case of Thornton Township, this mantle was taken up by a man named Joseph Soltis.

Born in Budapest, Hungary, Soltis owned a saloon in Joliet. Like so many gangsters, this uneducated man still had the insight to envision the opportunity presented with the passing of the Volstead Act. He moved to Chicago, specifically the Back of the Yards neighborhood. As its name indicated, Back of the Yards was/is located in an area loosely bounded by Pershing Road to the north, 55th Street to the south and Halsted Street and Daman Avenue to the east and west. At once a bustling area filled with first Irish, German and later some Lithuanian and Slovakian immigrants who toiled in the stockyards, it was also characterized by the pollution, disease and overpowering stench of the thousands of carcasses strewn about nearby on a daily basis.

As a melting pot for new immigrants, it was a hotbed of gangs and crime, beginning with the Irish gangs in the late nineteenth century. In the book *The Gangs of New York*, a character named "Bill the Butcher" held sway in the Five Points area of New York. Chicago's Back of the Yards was filled with real butchers who toiled with sharp knives and cleavers sixty hours a week. To settle a dispute with a carving knife would not seem out of the ordinary. During the 1880s, the Irish gangs, allied with crooked politicians, preyed on the new eastern European immigrants.

Back of the Yards is located south of what was originally the Levy and South Loop area, controlled by Jim Colosimo, Johnny Torrio and later Al Capone. Other gangsters in the area included the O'Donnell and Shelton Gangs. With its violent history and Slovakian population, Soltis fit right in. He quickly allied himself with the local Irish gangsters, including a political hack named John "Dingbat" O'Berta and later Frank McErlane. In an era known for violent sociopaths and killers, McErlane's penchant for cruel violence alarmed even the most hardened of gangsters. He is credited for introducing the Thompson machine gun, aka the Tommy gun, to gangland Chicago. A severe alcoholic, it is said that his penchant for cruelty and violence grew with each drink, of which there were many. With both political clout and gun-toting muscle, Soltis was able to keep control over Chicago's Southwest Side. He gradually moved west out of Back of the Yards and was able to keep independent from Capone's control through the early 1920s. In 1926, Soltis entered into a gang war with the O'Donnell and Shelton Gangs. The gang war effectively weakened these smaller gangs, and Capone saw an opportunity to move in. Soltis read the tea leaves and sought out a meeting with Capone.

"At this point Soltis went to Capone to propose a truce, and in the end Soltis ended up working for Capone hauling liquor, which probably saved his life," Howell said. "One of the places 'Al' sent him was to Thornton, at the old Bielfeldt brewery."

Soltis, who was also known as "Saltis" in many accounts, ran truckloads of beer from Thornton to Chicago. The building was disguised as a soda pop plant, and it is likely that local law enforcement was on the payroll. Capone was known to occasionally stop by, and at one time a leather chair belonging to Al's brother Ralph Capone sat inside the brewery. As Prohibition continued, Capone and Soltis continued to thrive and become famous (or infamous). So much so that when the first Public Enemies list was formed, Capone was ranked no. 1, while Soltis was slotted at a still impressive no. 9. Capone's conviction for tax evasion and the end of Prohibition mean that Thornton returned to being a legitimate brewery. According to Howell, Soltis did attempt to keep control of the brewery. "'Pollack Joe' Soltis apparently put a bid on the brewery, and when his bid was rejected he threatened that there would be 'no more brewery,' but apparently nothing ever came of it," Howell said.

Thornton Brewing returned to being a legitimate brewery, and Soltis moved to northern Wisconsin. Photos taken during the heyday of his gangsterdom, many provided by Soltis's grandson and Howell's former partner Steve Soltis, present Soltis as a gentleman, but Howell paints a different picture. Like Johnny Rocco, played by Edward G. Robinson in the film *Key Largo*, Soltis apparently spent much of the 1940s holed up in Wisconsin (not Florida), pining for the glory days of Prohibition. They never came back. "Soltis ended up impoverished," Howell says. "He died in 1947 and in a photo taken before he died he had teeth missing and a bandage around his head. Somebody said he got into a fight in a saloon where a bandleader broke a guitar over his head."

In the meantime, the Thornton Brewery recovered and went back into operation brewing real and possibly better beer with mixed results. "From 1933 to 1936, John Kubine took over the brewery," Howell says. "From 1937 to 1940, it was the Illinois Brewery, Frederick's Brewery from 1940 to 1948, and from 1948 to 1950 it became the McAvery Brewery. Its last run was as the White Bear Brewery, which was run from 1950 to 1957 run by a Lithuanian immigrant named Joe Sadauskas."

But just as Chicago's small and mid-sized breweries began to falter in the early days of television, the brewery closed circa 1957. In the following years, it was used as a residence and auto body shop and even a machine shop. Thus it lost its title as Chicagoland's oldest continuous brewery. It was reborn as a restaurant, the Brewery Bar and Grill, in 1990, but in August 1992 it was closed in a raid by the Metropolitan Enforcement Group. But like the artesian springs that flow underneath, the life of the Thornton Brewery and its connection to alcohol could not be quelled. For years, Andy Howell had been a home brewer and distiller. After graduating from Chicago's Columbia College, Howell worked at several jobs but always steered toward becoming an entrepreneur. By then, the microbrewery craze had long hit Chicago. Howell, who is also an avid historian, began to try to combine his two hobbies.

"I was researching historical buildings in Illinois, specifically breweries or alcohol-related products," Howell says. "I found out about the old Bielfeldt Brewery. It was on our radar, and when we came out to look at the site, we fell in love with it."

Another stroke of good luck came when Howell met Jake Weiss. As the owner of a small apartment complex next door, Weiss had long had his eye on the brewery property. Weiss had income and loan collateral from his other properties. Howell had a knowledge of brewing, an appreciation for history and youthful energy. Howell "pitched him," and a partnership was formed.

The next three years could probably serve as a "model telling" of the stories of most young investors who end up opening breweries or distilleries. "We saw a little house down the street that went up for auction," Howell said. "So three guys moved in and worked day jobs while at night and on weekends we worked on restoring the building. Some of the construction we did on our own, and for other jobs we hired tradesmen."

The next chapter in the story involves Steve Soltis, as well as many of the elements of intrigue that encapsulate the history of alcohol in Chicago. In early 2017, media outlets including the *Chicago Tribune* and *Chicago Magazine* ran long interviews with Soltis. As he claimed to be the great-grandson of Joe Soltis, ledes with themes like "Gangsters Great Grandson to Follow in Footsteps by Opening Brewery" made for great copy.

The way Howell and Soltis met is hazy. Howell said that his connection to the family is through Joe Soltis's great-grandniece Josephine, to whom he is related through marriage. A Renaissance man and artist, Steve Soltis, along with Howell, Weiss and a fourth man, Micah Kibodeaux, a chef from New Orleans, cruised into 2017 with grand ideas for the brewery. Its plans for opening were met with much fanfare. But in many ways, the facts did not add up. One example may be the way Joe Soltis is depicted. In the *Chicago Magazine* interview, Steve claimed that his "great-grandfather" was also a Renaissance man, who broke horses for the U.S. Cavalry, loved books and art and befriended the Menominee Indians. Howell sees him as more of a thug, as evidenced by his depiction of him in his final years. But this is not the only time Soltis and Howell did not see eye to eye. Howell claimed that besides making for good copy in local media, Soltis often made politically incorrect and brazen comments, and he became wary of Soltis as potential host for a business mixing with customers every night. "Soltis was never a partner," Howell said. "And we were never able to verify that he was the great-grandson or even related to [Joe] Soltis."

Whatever the story may be, Steve Soltis is no longer a part of the business, vanishing like the water vapor that is created when distilling spirits. In the meantime, Howell continues to move forward on the operation. The name was changed from Soltis Family Spirits to the Thornton Distilling Company.

"Jake and I applied for a Distilled Spirits Plant, or DSP license, to produce spirits," Howell said.

During those formative years, Howell and his partners wavered between opening a brewery or a distillery, and Howell settled on a distillery. After purchasing the equipment and learning the fundamentals of distilling, in part through the Chicago workshops run by KOVAL's Sonat Birnecker Hart, Howell received his license and began to distill rum. As time went on, however, Howell found that much of his time had to be devoted to business meetings and promotions and hired Ari Klafter as his head distiller. Klafter holds an MSc degree in brewing and distilling from the Heriot-Watt School of Brewing and Distilling Sciences. Located in Edinburgh, Scotland, it is widely recognized as one of the finest programs for distilling science in the world. Klafter could have worked at almost any microbrewery but decided to go into distilling instead.

"With no slight to the craft of microbrewing and all the skill it takes, I find distilling, with all of its different products, grains, flavors, as well as the fact that it is more complicated and can even be dangerous if done by somebody who is not trained, to be more challenging," said Klafter, who is president of the Illinois Craft Distilling Association. In the past few years, microbrewing and opening a brewery had become so popular that it had begun to lose its aura. "Microbrewing isn't so unique anymore," Klafter said. "It's jumped the shark."

Spirits are aged in oak barrels. *Photo by author.*

Howell and Klafter began the process of producing their own line of distilled products. Given the moniker of Dead Drop Spirits after a bootlegging term for leaving barrels in a hidden location, Thornton currently produces Dead Drop Pecan whiskey, gin, dark rum, vodka, rye and pre-mixed Old Fashioned.

"The vodka and gin we produced more quickly," Howell said. "They do not require aging and are known in the trade as 'youthful spirits.' For the pecan whiskey we trim, cut and toast pecan staves provided by the last pecan farm in Illinois. It is then put in barrels and aged. The rum is made from molasses and sugar cane and aged for two years, and the rye is also aged in oak barrels for two years."

Thornton products can be purchased locally or nationally, but many prefer to enjoy them at the distillery itself. Thornton features Howell and his partners currently producing spirits including pecan whiskey, gin, spiced rum and single malt bourbon. They use the water from the spring-fed well in the basement, with a distilling capacity of fifty-three gallon barrels per day. These spirits are turned into cocktails, which customers at The Well sip either in the outdoor patio or at an indoor bar built alongside the nearly 150-year-old exposed brick of the original Thornton Brewery. It's a hot spot for locals and a destination for adventurous drinkers from nearby Chicago, and Howell is hoping to add one final link to the building's history. "We recently applied for a brewing license," he noted, "and we want to bring back the traditional styles of beer made at the Thornton, including lager and pilsner."

Native Americans; a Kinzie; German, Irish and Lithuanian brewers; spring water; draft horses; Prohibition; gangsters; dark years; and new life as a micro-distillery/brewery—the historic link between alcohol and Chicago continues, much of it contained at the former Thorntown Brewery, now called The Well at the Distillery.

The smaller bar area and patio feature a bar and small-scale restaurant, but the larger building also hosts private parties, weddings and corporate events. As customers enjoy their spirits and company, they are also walking in the same building and the same land that Native Americans, John H. Kinzie, John S. Bielfeldt, Joseph Soltis, Al Capone and thousands of horsemen, rail workers, truck drivers, friends, wives, girlfriends and others have walked on for more than 175 years. Almost all of them came there for the same reason: to enjoy alcohol and spirits.

KOVAL DISTILLERY AND TASTING ROOM

Distilling Returns to Chicago After 140 Years

Since about 1890, every sip of spirits taken in the city of Chicago was distilled outside the city. Just think of the millions upon millions of bottles, shots, glasses and gulps that must have been. But this all changed in 2008 with the opening of the KOVAL Distillery. But KOVAL did more than just end the century-plus "drought" of grain-to-bottle distilling in Chicago—it created an entirely new industry. In doing so, it also broke almost every single American stereotype associated with whiskey, distilling and the business of booze. First, there is the plant itself. When you walk into the KOVAL Distillery, you are met by an array of smells that overtake the senses. While there are towering stainless steel and copper stills and oak barrels, there is little smell of steel, oak or alcohol. Instead, the scent of grain, berries and other botanicals gives the plant an almost floral aura, as if you were in a meadow. The same is true for the tasting room. While many distilleries prefer a darker, tavern-like setting with a roughhewn feel, KOVAL features a sleek, modern décor filled with bright, smooth hardwoods illuminated by floor-to-ceiling windows. Then there is the whiskey itself, made 100 percent from grain to bottle. Through endless caricatures, cartoons and, yes, the TV show *Moonshiners*, the distillers of whiskey are generally portrayed as male, living in rural areas and dressed in coveralls or shabby suits with tattered hats; whether legal or not, they turn to liquor making as somewhat "outlaws." KOVAL is none of these.

Cofounder Robert Birnecker is from Washington, D.C., has a doctorate in political science and formerly worked in Washington as the deputy press

KOVAL founders Robert and Sonat Birnecker. *KOVAL Distilleries.*

secretary at the Austrian embassy. His wife, Sonat Birnecker Hart, has a doctorate degree and taught German cultural history and Jewish studies at the university level. The couple lived in an urban center and were looking toward a second career. They represent one of the best examples of twenty-first-century brewers and distillers who turned to the craft simply because they wanted change.

"In 2008, we were very much at a crossroads," Birnecker Hart said. "We were living in Washington, D.C., I was pregnant, and we were both looking for a new type of career where we could work together, preferably in our own business, where we would not have to commute, giving us more time to be together with each other and our children. At first we were thinking of a Viennese-style coffee house, but then we shifted our focus to bringing the distilling traditions of Robert's Austrian grandfather to Chicago because it would offer something new and fresh to the business scene of the city."

Her great-grandfather Emanual Loewnhertz was an electrical engineer and ran a factory in Chicago. Robert's grandfather Robert Schmied Sr. was a distiller who made award-winning cider and spirits, which he sold at restaurants in Upper Austria.

The couple then proceeded to break another distilling stereotype. In rural areas, illegal stills are often hidden in the woods. Legally licensed operations are still located in remote areas close to a source of water and grain and away from major population centers. KOVAL is located in the heart of Chicago's Ravenswood area. Once heavily working class with light industry, primarily along Ravenswood Avenue, the 1990s saw a drastic change. If you needed to explain the urban gentrification and "yuppie" movement of the 1990s, Ravenswood would be a prime example. The area was not only working class, but there were also many years when it became a battleground between the largely white street gangs of Uptown to the north and the primarily Hispanic gangs from Lakeview to the south. But this all changed. In fact, there was a period around 2010 when Chicago's Mayor Rahm Emanuel, Illinois governor Rod Blagojevich and Lisa Madigan, the state attorney general, all lived about a mile from the KOVAL plant. Real estate was no longer cheap. But the couple really liked the space, and the aldermen liked their plan. Still, they needed a large, commercial space with lofty ceilings, large doors and loading docks, all on a limited budget.

"Joe Hayes [a local realtor and landowner] showed us a space and we thought it was too expensive so we asked to split it in half. He thought for a minute and simply agreed to give us the whole space for a very reasonable price."

Unlike some of the infamous distillers in Chicago's "business," KOVAL did everything legally and above board. In doing so, it navigated the miles of bureaucratic red tape and actually created an entirely new set of laws and regulations for Chicago distilling. "We had followed the federal and state rules, we were ordering all our materials to distill and we were ready to go," Birnecker Hart said. "The city sent someone by the distillery twice, but they didn't know what to do. This had never happened in the city's memorable past, as there was nothing in the codes since 1934 and at the time, we only were required to have a state and federal license. There just was not a city license we could even apply for, as we were not allowed to retail on-site in the beginning."

Birnecker Hart met with local Alderman Eugene Schulter, State Representative Greg Harris and State Senator Heather Steans. After researching laws in Wisconsin and then other states, Steans came up with what would eventually become the business landscape for craft distillers in Illinois. As most know, gears turn very slowly in government.

"We were running out of money," Birnecker Hart said. "I was pregnant again, but I really had no choice but to start driving down to Springfield [the capital] and try to get the process moving, because I knew that this would make a big difference in sales."

The result of KOVAL's efforts, the first Illinois Craft Distilleries Bill, afforded distillers the ability to offer tours, tastings and retail on-site, bringing Illinois more in line with some of the other states in the nation that were helping to support the growing industry of craft distilling. The bill, SB2797, which was amended in 2016, allows craft distillers to manufacture up to 100,000 gallons per year on premises and sell their product nation and worldwide. With this bill and the work of Birnecker Hart, the foundation for the distilling industry in Chicago was laid.

"The bill revolutionized the industry," she said. "In Illinois, brew pub business was already booming, but with this bill a lot of people became interested in distilling as well, since different business models became possible beyond manufacturing alone."

Above: Founded in 2008, KOVAL was the first large, legal commercial distillery to be established in Chicago in almost 150 years. *KOVAL Distilleries.*

Right: Sonat Birnecker beside one of KOVAL's many stills. *KOVAL Distilleries.*

But the couple and the group at KOVAL did not just stop with creating an industry for themselves. Together, they almost became the godmother and godfather to many of Chicago's distilleries and other such businesses across the nation. In doing so, they defeated yet another infamous Chicago alcohol business stereotype, that of the cutthroat "gangster" willing to do anything to "wipe out" the competition. Instead, the Birneckers taught classes and workshops in distilling and also gave advice and support to bolster those who wanted to enter the industry. More than 3,500 people nationwide and worldwide have attended these classes and workshops. In Chicago, their impact is even greater.

"Robert has become one of the world's leading distillery consultants and has worked on innovations in both the automation systems for distilling as well as the still designs. He has also done a lot for the home team. Through our consulting arm, Kothe Distilling Technologies, we have helped set up FEW Distilleries and the Chicago Distilling Company, among many others in the Midwest," Birnecker Hart said. "The owners or employees from CH Distillery, Letherbee and Blaum Bros. have also attended our classes. Overall we have helped to set up over 200 turnkey operations in places as far away as Uganda, Japan and Israel."

KOVAL now makes a full line of spirits. *KOVAL Distilleries.*

Yet just when the Birneckers had seemingly cleared all their bureaucratic hurdles and were distributing spirits both locally, nationally and internationally to more than fifty-five export markets, there came another, even more ominous crisis: COVID-19. This deadly virus wreaked havoc on almost all portions of the American economy. In the spring of 2020, the crisis of this completely unknown, deadly virus loomed even larger. With their close ties to Europe, the Birneckers were closely monitoring the situation in Italy, the first European country to suffer a great onslaught of COVID-19. In talking with Italian distillers, they learned that in this crisis, the alcohol was better suited for medical purposes.

"We wanted to switch to making hand sanitizer," Birnecker Hart said. "But at that time it was not legal. We were not allowed to use the alcohol for any purpose other than distilling."

The KOVAL team brought this up to the local officials, aldermen and more, but this was a federal issue. But as the crisis raged, local and national politicians, including Fifth District congressman Mike Quigley, found a way to move forward.

"We got the go-ahead on Thursday night, and on Friday we were making hand sanitizer," Birnecker Hart said. "On Monday, we were distributing it to local police, fire and workers in hospitals and nursing homes. Almost immediately we were getting hundreds of phone calls; I mean we got so many calls that we basically worked with our necks pressed against our cellphones twenty-four hours a day. People began to donate money to help make more hand sanitizer to donate to the community. All the breweries began giving us beer so we could distill it and make it into hand sanitizer. Everybody pitched in, and it was a very uplifting and heartwarming experience."

As the pandemic is hopefully continuing to wind down as of 2022, KOVAL's distilling, bottling and shipping are once again literally going "full steam." All 100 percent organic, kosher and made entirely on-site, some of their feature products include their bourbon, which won a Gold Medal at the International Whisky Competition; rye, which captured Best International Whiskey;

A KOVAL Old Fashioned. *KOVAL Distilleries.*

and Four Grain Whiskey. The company also makes an exquisite series of gins, including Dry Gin, Barreled Gin and its Cranberry Gin Liqueur, which also won a Gold Medal from the International Review of Spirits. All these medals in addition to creating an entire new Chicago industry and breaking almost all distilling stereotypes in the process!

"We try to do things in a way that elevates everything," Birnecker Hart said. "We want to have the finest spirits, classes, tours and a comfortable yet elegant tasting room and outdoor patio—all kind of like Chicago itself, beautiful but also down to earth. Chicago can compete favorably with any city in the world, and so can our spirits."

THE NEW GENERATION OF CHICAGO DISTILLERIES

W hile they will never be able to equal the production of the Peoria Whiskey Trust or those of the existing distilleries in Kentucky or Tennessee, there is a new boom in the distilling of small-batch, craft whiskey distillers in Chicagoland. Opening after the birth of so many craft breweries, they now form an industry unto itself, attracting both locals and tourists and creating a new craft whiskey industry in the Chicago area. These craft whiskey buyers represent a new breed of whiskey drinkers and purchasers. Intent on purity and quality, these discerning drinkers are doing for spirits what farm-to-table restaurants have done for the dining industry. There are other distilleries in the Chicagoland area, and more may open during the proceeding months and years. While KOVAL has already been profiled, here is a handy guide to the stories behind Chicago's most notable craft distilleries.

FEW DISTILLERS

Located in Evanston, Illinois, a city that was "dry" until 1972 and just a few blocks south of Frances Willard's former home and WCTU museum, FEW Spirits seems to defy the tradition of the suburb just north of Chicago's city limits. FEW Spirits was also awarded "Craft Whiskey of the Year" by *Whiskey Advocate* and has won numerous medals, awards and ribbons at craft whiskey festivals worldwide.

FEW distilleries is located a few blocks south of Frances Willard's WCTU home in Evanston, Illinois. *Photo by author.*

"We are located in Evanston, but that has little or nothing to do with the fact that Frances Willard lived here, or in the past the city did not only have brewing or distilling. You could not even buy liquor here until 1972," said Paul Hletko, founder and distiller of the company. "It is simply where I live, and I am close to home and able to walk my kids to school."

Like many in this new age of brewers and distillers, Hletko bounced around from job to job until creating and nurturing his dream. "I have always been a creative person," Hletko noted. "I play guitar and for a while designed and built guitar pedals [apparatus used to enhance the effects of the instrument] and owned a very small record label that specialized in house music."

Hletko's distilling roots lay in central Europe, specifically Czech Republic, as the art of making home alcohol has been passed down through the family, skipping a generation. "My grandfather owned a brewery in [what was then] Czechoslovakia," Hletko said. "It was successful, but when the Nazis came, they confiscated the brewery and murdered many members of his family. He survived, but after they took over the brewery it was pretty much gone. This is what helped to inspire me to take it to the professional level."

In perhaps the only thing that resembles the Prohibition stills of the gangsters, Hletko found a faded, white brick building at the end of an alley off Chicago Avenue in Evanston. The building formerly housed a "chop shop," or a place where stolen cars were disassembled and sold for parts. Having no experience in craft distilling, he took a class, got some advice from the people at KOVAL and then went to work making whiskey. "It was an entrepreneurial challenge getting the equipment, buying the grain and beginning to make whiskey," Hletko said. "Ten years ago nobody knew what craft spirits were, and now we make up 5 percent of the market."

Besides the award-winning whiskey, FEW is also known for its distinctive labels, which definitely represent Chicago history. The bourbon whiskey boasts a simple red-ink label that features a drawing of the Statue of the Republic, the iconic gold figure that welcomed the 28 million visitors to the Chicago World's Fair/Columbian Exposition

Its most popular label commemorates the Statue of the Republic, here at Chicago World's Fair, 1893. *Few Distilleries.*

of 1893. The rye label, done in the same simple ink but blue, is a drawing of the giant Ferris wheel that also came to symbolize the event. The copy on FEW's website also pays homage to the Fair:

> *Also known as the Columbian Exposition, the 1983 World's Fair took place in Chicago, Illinois. It represented the dawn of modernism and introduced our nation to phosphorescent lights, moving walkways, an electrically powered water fountain and the invention of the Ferris Wheel. It was even the launching ground of a notable brand of juicy chewing gum and a brand of beer that was awarded a first place blue ribbon. Both are still around today.*

"We are a Chicago distillery, and in so many ways the 1893 World's Fair still symbolizes Chicago. It was a big deal," Hletko said. "It made Chicago what it is today, it was a rebirth after the fire, represents one of the stars on the flag, and actually changed not only the way the world looks at Chicago, but the world itself."

At the end of their brief description, FEW pays homage to Wrigley's gum and Pabst Blue Ribbon beer, two products introduced at the Fair. Yet in his remarks, Hletko expressed that he wanted to produce an alternative to what was then the major American whiskey brands, now mostly owned by worldwide conglomerates. It was this disdain that, as well as the ability to be an entrepreneur, has driven Hletko and FEW to its position today.

FEW is the second-best-selling craft bourbon and has gained national and international acclaim, winning gold medals at the International Review of Spirits (2014) and a Best Bourbon, Double Gold Medal in 2019. FEW Rye won a double gold medal at the San Francisco World Spirits Competition and was awarded "Best in Class" at the 2020 Whiskies of the World Festival.

Hletko is proud of these accomplishments but is even prouder of the team he has built around him. "Our spirits have won many awards and critical acclaim, but I am most proud of the team I have assembled around me," he noted. "I would like to thank many individuals like Riley Henderson, Steven Kaplan and all the amazingly talented people at FEW who have made this whole business a very cool, awesome and inspiring adventure."

CHICAGO DISTILLING COMPANY

In many ways, the Chicago Distilling Company represents the many new microbreweries, brewpubs and small distilleries that have cropped up

Chicago Distilling produces and serves spirits in house. *Photo by author.*

around the nation. In fact, many small and mid-sized towns now boast, at the top of their tourist "things to do," that they have a microbrewery or small distillery. Like at many microbreweries and brewpubs, spirits drinkers buy and consume their products on-site in its tasting room/lounge.

Chicago Distilling is located on a strip of bars and nightclubs in Chicago's trendy Wicker Park neighborhood. While distilleries like KOVAL and FEW distribute nation and worldwide to drinkers of all ages and many races, Chicago Distilling Company is located in Chicago's neighborhood known for its ongoing gentrification. It is also the home neighborhood for many "hipsters," known for riding bikes, growing beards, boasting tattoos and enjoying craft beer. Chicago Distilling caters to both groups. Brothers Vic and Jay DiPrizio and Jay's wife, Noelle, run the company. It was started in 2010 and distills very small batches of vodka, gin, malt whiskey, rye whiskey, white whiskey and even absinthe. The operative word here is *small* or even *very small* batches. Its trademarks are Blind Tiger Bourbon, which is a takeoff on the Prohibition-era bars known as "blind pigs," and Stouted Whiskey. It also features barrel-aged vodka and gin, which are stored in oak barrels.

Chicago Distilling offers tours and tastings, and besides its regular spirits, it is known for its craft cocktails. A trip to Chicago Distilling offers the benefits of a local lounge and the benefits of spirits made on-site.

Maplewood Distilleries

Located in the Logan Square Neighborhood, Maplewood is the first location to serve both as a brewery and distillery. Opened in 2014, Maplewood's sales have expanded to include Indiana, Wisconsin and Kansas. House-made spirits include Maplewood Vodka, Maplewood Coffee Liqueur, Maplewood Spruce Gin, Maplewood Brewers Gin, Maplewood White Rum, Wheated Whiskey and an even larger selection of craft beers, ales and IPAs made on-site.

Rhine Hall Distillery

Like with KOVAL, this family-run distillery has its roots in Austria and Germany, specializing in fruit-based brandy, schnapps and traditional fruit brandies called Eau De Vies. Opened in 2013, Rhine Hall, named after an ice rink in Austria, is run by the father-and-daughter team of Charles and Jenny Solberg. Located in the Fulton Street Corridor, it is not far from the CH Distillery and Wolf Point. The fruits used in the product are all sourced from the Great Lakes region, and each bottle contains about twenty-five pounds of fruit. Rhine Hall offers a tasting room, tours, cocktail classes and other events.

CH Distillery Tasting Room and Cocktail Bar

As covered in previous chapters, CH Distillery purchased the rights to Malört and now distills, produces and has sole rights to the product. But CH is more than just Malört. Founded in 2013, "CH" stands both for Chicago and the fundamental compounds in alcohol: carbon and hydrogen. The vodka and Malört are made in a fifty-thousand-square-foot facility that sits on 2.5 acres of land located on Chicago's near South Side, near the old Schoenhofen Brewery, which is now a landmark. The distillery still maintains its gritty, industrial heritage. Not so with the CH Distillery Tasting Room and Cocktail Bar. Located at 564 West Randolph, it is just west of the Loop and very close to Chicago's ultra-hip Halsted and Randolph restaurant corridor. Besides cocktails made

The Tasting Room and Cockail Bar of CH Distillery, makers of Malört bourbon and other spirits. *Photo by author.*

from CH spirits, it also offers an extensive food menu. Many of these foods are based on drink recipes, including Key Gin Feta, Ancho Whiskey Duck Tacos and Drunken Mussels. House-made spirits include Malört bourbon and CH rum, gin and vodka. All are offered in a sleek, modern facility that is sure to cater to tourists as well as craft spirit aficionados.

WOLF POINT DISTILLING

And so we come full circle. Chicago spirits, and in many ways the city itself, began at Wolf Point—a place where the North, South and Main Branches of the Chicago River meet. Trappers, Native Americans and the city's earliest settlers started fires, laid down blankets, had a bite to eat and drank spirits to warm up. Wolf Distilling celebrates this tradition in many ways. Its logo is patterned after the Chicago Y, the municipal symbol of the three rivers meeting. The label of its trademark bourbon boasts a drawing of a wolf in front of a campfire. The co-owners are Victoria Polvino and Pavlos Dafnis, and the head distiller is Steve Dethrow. Dafnis, a former sheet metal worker, and Polvino are part of the tradition of the millennial generation who tried various jobs but found creativity, independence and adventure in distilling.

The new distillery also has a tie with Chicago tradition, albeit more recent. It is located at 215 North Laflin Street, close to the old Fulton Markets. This

Wolf Point Distilling takes Chicago distilling back full circle to Wolf Point. *Photo by author.*

was a semi-industrial neighborhood that featured small slaughterhouses and meat distributorships, wholesale fruit and vegetable warehouses and Chicago's old fish houses, where fresh fish was sold in giant steel tubs packed with ice. It is also not far from the old Skid Row.

The names and the products themselves all revolve around Chicago history. Florence Field Gin is named after the Chicago philanthropist who donated the lions to the Art Institute. O'Leary's Cow Cinnamon Vodka is named after the woman who allegedly began the Great Chicago Fire. Then there is the Wolf Point Bourbon—full-bodied and smoky, with that bit of heat that hits the back of your throat on the way down. Like the label featuring the wolf and campfire, it brings back a bit of the taste of those early, early days of Chicago, when wolves howled, campfires burned and Potawatomis and other Native Americans, trappers and roughhewn men decided to lie down, rest and have a bite of smoked salmon, game and bread to go with a distilled spirit. Distilled spirits have been an important part of Chicago history since the first days of trappers and traders, and Wolf Point Distilling brings this history full circle. In its previous 175 years of existence, it was products by early distillers, bathtub gin made by gangsters or rectifiers making sweet brandy. Now this new wave of producers is adding yet another chapter to the long history of spirits: "Distilled in Chicago."

BIBLIOGRAPHY

Andreas, A.T. *History of Chicago*. Chicago: A.T. Andreas, 1886.

Asbury, Herbert. *The Gangs of Chicago: An Informal History of the Chicago Underworld*. New York: Alfred A. Knopf, 1940.

Bohlman, Rachael. "The Temperance Movement." The Electronic Encyclopedia of Chicago. Chicago Historical Society, 2005.

Bohlman, Rachel Elizabeth. "Drunken Husbands, Drunken State: The Woman's Christian Temperance Union's Challenge to American Families and Public Communities in Chicago, 1874–1920." Thesis, University of Iowa, 1922.

Brachear, Manya. Obituary, Peter Kovler. *Chicago Tribune*, August 24, 2003.

Chicago Distilling Company. www.chicagodistilling.com.

The Chicago History Museum Online. *Map of the South Side Levee*. https://www.chicagohistory.org.

Chicago Tribune. "Mark Beaubien, One of Chicago's First Settlers Dying in Kankakee: Biographical Sketch of Historic Tavern Keeper and Fiddler." March 25, 1881.

———. Obituary, Jerome Leavitt. July 9, 1998.

Dorsett, Lyle W. *Billy Sunday and the Redemption of Urban America*. Grand Rapids, MI: W.B. Eerdmans, 1991.

Enright, Laura L. *Chicago's Most Wanted: The Top Ten Book of Murderous Mobsters, Midway Monsters, and Windy City Oddities*. Dulles, VA: Potomac Books Inc., 2005.

Fire Engineering. "Chicago 'Skid Row' Hotel Fire Results in 29 Casualties." Reprinted from fireengineering.com.

Gleason, William. *The Liquid Cross of Skid Row*. Milwaukee, WI: Bruce Publishing, 1966.

Graves, Dan. "Beer Garden Became Pacific Garden Mission." Christianity, May 3, 2010. https://www.christianity.com/church/church-history/timeline/1801-1900/beer-garden-became-pacific-garden-mission-11630589.html.

Hishtory. "Chicago and Prohibition." February 12, 2017. http://www.hishtory.com/blog-1/2017/2/12/chicago-and-prohibition.

Historical Film Classics—International Historic Films. "Skid Row: Chicago's Madison Street in the 1940s."

Illinois History Journal. "The Green Tree Tavern, Lake and West and Water Streets, Chicago Illinois: A Firsthand Account of an Overnight Stay." Digital Research Library of Illinois History Journal. drloihjournal.blogspot.com/2016/12/the-green-tree-tavern-lake-and-west.html.

Jones, Chris. "Hope Abelson, 1910–2006." *Chicago Tribune*, September 3, 2006.

Jones, Fernando. "Memoirs of Old Chicago, Fernando Jones Relates His Experiences in the Earliest Days of This Present City." *Chicago Tribune*, October 10, 1897.

Jurkowski, Vickie Snow. "Soltis Family Distills Spirits Amid Remnants of South Side Brewing Lore." *Daily Southtown/Chicago Tribune*, March 29, 2018.

Kogan, Herman, and Lloyd Wendt. *Lords of the Levee: The Story of Bathhouse John and Hinky Dink*. Evanston, IL: Northwestern University Press, 2005. Originally published 1943.

Lawler, Moira. "Gangster's Great Grandson Returns to Thornton Distillery." *Chicago Magazine* (May 19, 2017).

Meier, Tiffany A., and D. Bradford Hunt. "Shelterforce Online: Public Dollars and Private Interests, How Skid Row Fought Back Against Chicago's Private Developers." *Chicago Coalition for the Homeless*, no. 134 (March/April 2004). http://www.chicagohomeless.org/shelterforce-online-public-dollars-and-private-interests-how-skid-row-fo.

Meyer, Erin. Obituary, Fred Cooper. *Chicago Tribune*, May 1, 2011.

Ness, Eliot, and Oscar Fraley. *The Untouchables*. Cutchogue, NY: Buccaneer Press, 1957.

Nolan, Mike. "Historic Thornton Brewery Building Getting New Life as Distillery." *Daily Southtown/Chicago Tribune*, February 23, 2017.

Northwestern University. "Homicide in Chicago, 1870–1930." http://homicide.northwestern.edu/database/3058/?page=Object%20id%20.

Pierce, Bessie Louise. *A History of Chicago: From Town to City*. Vol. 2. New York: Knopf, 1940.

Prohibition: An Interactive History. "Bootleggers and Bathtub Gin." https://prohibition.themobmuseum.org/the-history/the-prohibition-underworld/bootleggers-and-bathtub-gin.

Rothman, Lilly. "The History of Alcohol Poisoning Includes and Unusual Culprit—The US Government." *Time*, January 15, 2015.

Sazerac. "Medley." http://www.sazerac.com/medley.aspx.

Slokum, William J. "Skid Row USA." *Collier's*, September 3, 1949, via *Time*.

Stephens, Calev. *Dayton Business Journal*, August 11, 2018.

Sunday, Billy. *The Sawdust Trail: Billy Sunday in His Own Words*. Iowa City: University of Iowa Press, 2005.

Sweeney, Brigid. "Wirtz Family in Deal to Create 12 Billion Dollar Liquor Distributor." *Crain's Chicago Business*, November 20, 2017.

Trotter, Greg. "Rocky Wirtz's Breakthru Beverage to Merge with Texas-Based Firm, Becoming $12 Billion Liquor Distributor." *Chicago Tribune*, November 20, 2017.

Waxman, Naomi. "Incoming West Loop Distillery Tells a Chicago Tale in Each Sip." *Chicago Eater*, December 7, 2021.

Weinberg, Mark. *Career Misconduct: The Story of Bill Wirtz's Greed, Corruption and Betrayal of Black Hawks Fans*. Chicago: Blueline Publishing, 2000.

Whiskey University. "Oscar Getz." https://www.whiskeyuniv.com/g-oscar-getz.

Wikipedia. "Joseph Saltis." wikipedia.org/wiki/Joseph Saltis.

Willard, Frances Elizabeth. *Home Protection Manual*. New York: The Independent Office, 1879.

Wittenmeyer, Anne. *History of the Woman's Temperance Crusade: A Complete Official History of the Wonderful Uprising of the Christian Woman of the United States Against Liquor Traffic, Which Culminated in the Gospel Temperance Movement*. Philadelphia, PA: Office of Christian Women, 1878.

Wolf Point Distilling. www.wolfpointdistilling.com.

Interviews

Birnecker, Sonat. Interview with author, April 2022.

———. Interview with author, February 2022.

Hletco, Paul. Interview with author, April 2022.

Howell, Andrew. Interview with author, February 1, 2022.

———. Interview with author, October 3, 2018.

Howell, Andy. Interview with author, August 24, 2018.

Kaplan, Jacob. Interview with author, January 16, 2019.

Olsen, Janet. Interview with author, WCTU Museum, Evanston Illinois, December 30, 2017.

Pulaski, Frank. Interview with author, July 2012.

Schecter, Jeffery. Interview with author, Chicago, January 2 and 12, 2019.

Stratton, Cleo Brown. Interview with author, Miller Beach, Indiana, July 23, 2018.

ABOUT THE AUTHOR

David Witter is a Chicago-based author who has written four books: *Oldest Chicago I*, *Oldest Chicago II*, *Chicago Magic: A History of Stagecraft and Spectacle* and *Distilled in Chicago: A History*. His writing on Chicago has appeared in many publications, including *New City*, *The Chicago Reader* and the *Washington Post*.